Home Based Jobs

Jobs

Work From Home and Make Money Online

(Achieve Financial Freedom and Passive Income in the New Economy)

Maurice Smith

Published By **Ryan Princeton**

Maurice Smith

Home Based Jobs: Work From Home and Make Money Online (Achieve Financial Freedom and Passive Income in the New Economy)

ISBN   978-1-77485-995-7

No part of this guidebook shall be reproduced in any form without permission in writing from the publisher except in the case of brief quotations embodied in critical articles or reviews.

Legal & Disclaimer

The information contained in this ebook is not designed to replace or take the place of any form of medicine or professional medical advice. The information in this ebook has been provided for educational & entertainment purposes only.

The information contained in this book has been compiled from sources deemed reliable, and it is accurate to the best of the Author's knowledge; however, the Author cannot guarantee its accuracy and validity and cannot be held liable for any errors or omissions. Changes are periodically made to this book. You must consult your doctor or get professional medical advice before using any of the suggested remedies, techniques, or information in this book.

Table Of Contents

Chapter 1: What Are The Prospects Of Working From Home With Covid-19?

The Pew Research Center found that only 7% of American workers had the opportunity of working at home prior the outbreak of Covid-19 pandemic. Based on data from National Compensation Survey, this report was written by the Pew Research Center.

Now, millions of people have adapted to working from their spare rooms, kitchen tables and homes as a result office closures and stay at-home orders. The Coronavirus pandemic radically altered the workplace culture. But will this continue for the foreseeable?

Let's take a look at the reasons it took for a widespread pandemic in order to move many working environments from remote locations. We will also examine the possible future benefits of this new method.

Why was it that businesses were not keen to allow employees work from home before the Covid-19 outbreak?

Many organizations have hesitated to accept workers working from home. The reason is many, some of which are:

1. Many employers fear that productivity will drop. Employers worried that their employees wouldn't achieve as much or would lose valuable time if they weren't supervised.

Employers were concerned, too, that employees might not be able to communicate effectively between themselves and their coworkers.

They believed it was too complicated to switch to remote work.

Another cause for concern was that it required significant investment in new software, technologies and hardware to make remote work possible.

Many companies were prevented from changing to a remote-working model by these concerns and others. Many organizations couldn't resist the temptation to switch to remote work models when the COVID-19 pandemic erupted.

Why the work of a team will continue in the foreseeable near future

Although many businesses have now switched to telecommuting in order to follow the stay-at-home orders issued during the pandemic, will these tendencies still be present? Will we continue to telecommute, even when it's unnecessary?

There are many reasons that telecommuting will remain viable after COVID-19.

1. Organizations have invested in it

Covid-19 Pandemic forced organizations to set up the processes, resources, and technology their employees need in order to work effectively at home. This likely included purchasing new software and technology, creating new routines and scheduling, and creating workflows.

The fact that they have made a significant investment in time and money to create the model will ensure that they continue to follow it once normalcy returns. The system has just been created, so why not capitalize on it?

One of the biggest benefits of working remotely is the fact that you can enjoy lower costs and more advantages as your company grows. An organization can grow by creating a circulating workforce.

2. It is a healthier choice

Working remotely can help to prevent spreading diseases. This includes COVID-19. It also refers to other colds, influenza, or other conditions.

Many office workers are compelled even when they are sick to report to work.

Work environments will seek to reduce the incidence of sick workers being forced to report to work by placing more emphasis on collective and collective health.

Stanford's carbon emissions calculator shows that an employee with a 30 mile commute to work will produce 330lbs of carbon dioxide each month. That's almost four thousand pounds per annum. It is possible to eliminate these carbon emissions by working from home. You will also save fuel costs.

3. It's Better For the Environment

If more organizations adopt a work at home model, the environment will see big improvements.

Stanford's carbon emission calculator calculates that workers who commute 30 miles on average per day will emit 330lbs carbon each month. That's nearly 4,000 lbs per year! Telecommuting instantly will eliminate carbon emissions (and save you money on gas!)

Furthermore, it would not be a good idea to waste scarce resources or land on large office buildings if everyone is working remotely. We could make our homes double as workplaces, and use the office space to serve different purposes.

4. It's great for the happiness of employees

The happiness of employees is another reason that working remotely may prove to be a good idea. Happier employees will increase productivity and be more loyal to your company.

Owl Labs released "The Global State of Remote Work" to show that full-time remote employees are happier with their jobs. This is 30% more than workers who work on site. On the whole, however, working from home can result in a better balance between work and life, as well as less stress.

An employee can have a lot of fun even if it isn't cold driving to work. They can instead get a good night's sleep, have a warm breakfast at home, and log into work while wearing their favourite fluffy slippers.

5. It helps you save money

A lot of businesses make decisions without fully considering the reality. It is worth considering how much business can save using remote work systems.

The company will save money on office space as well as office supplies, electricity, computer equipment, and any other expenses that are necessary to keep the business running. Only a few people are required on the site, which reduces land costs. Business can reduce overhead, allowing them to invest capital elsewhere.

This will allow your team to be strong and excel in their respective fields.

A flexible policy that allows employees to work from home attracts more talent. If word gets out, your employees will feel at ease working from wherever they choose. This could make your company more appealing to potential employees.

6. It allows businesses to recruit more talented employees

One of the biggest benefits to working remotely is that your options for recruiting are not limited to your area. You can hire the best person for the position regardless of where they are located. This will allow for you to build a strong global workforce of professionals who are the best in the field.

Flexible work from home arrangements attract skilled workers. Your employees should be able to work from anywhere they want. This can increase the attractiveness of your organization to higher-quality talent.

7. It creates Opportunities to Diversity

There are amazing opportunities to enhance diversity in the workplace by working from home. Online work is more relaxed because it doesn't discriminate or hostilities.

Remote work makes recruiting top talent easier from around the world, giving your staff a global outlook. You can recruit your team members anywhere and discrimination is reduced. The emphasis is placed on the productivity of remote workers, rather than their appearance, gender, age, and ethnicity.

Conclusion: Even though we have the option to return to our offices at any time, we should question whether this is the right thing for us. Working from home has many benefits that we should be aware of.

Remote working could be the solution we have been looking for and it might even replace the need to work in an office.

Chapter 2: How To Make A Home Office

Being able to work remotely can be quite a challenge, especially for those who are used working in offices. You'll find helpful tips in this section on organizing your home office to make it more productive.

How to Create Your Home Office from Scratch

If you're currently working from home, it's time for you to create your own home office.

The options are endless. You can choose from a simple desk to place in your corner or an outdoor structure.

You will find some great tips to help you set up your home office.

Start building your home office space if either you're already working remotely or you plan to soon join the work-at-home group. You have many choices when it comes time to decide where your home office should be set up. Maybe you want to place it in an open-air building, or maybe you prefer to use a small desk in a corner.

Remote workers are known for being more productive than the average worker. A home office that is perfect allows you to work more efficiently, giving you the best chance to become one of these remote workers.

Why should you have a Home Office?

What is the point of having a private office to work from home? Maybe you're content with just working from your couch.

Even though you can work from any room in your home, there is a certain benefit to having a designated work area.

Remote workers have a high level of productivity. If you are looking to be a highly productive remote worker, you will need a home office that is well-designed.

1. A Home Office helps to create boundaries between personal life and work

The inability to create boundaries between personal life and work is a major problem for remote workers. This problem can easily be solved if you have a dedicated workspace in your home.

As simple as this may sound, getting up from the chair in your office and walking into your home office allows you to distinguish between being busy working and being home. This helps to avoid the stress of feeling like you work all day.

It can also help improve your professional image. Do you want your boss, clients, or team members to be able to view your private home? Instead, would you rather that they see a well-designed home office in the background?

2. A Home Office that's well designed can reduce distractions

It is likely that you will be working at home with children. The constant interruptions can hinder your productivity. But having your own office will help you establish boundaries when they are necessary.

To improve your productivity, make sure you have all the necessary supplies and equipment in your home office. To reduce disruptions and prevent wanderers from entering your office, keep office supplies, printers and other items close-by.

3. Your body will benefit from a comfortable workplace.

The posture and alignment of your body can be affected if you spend long hours on the sofa or bed, slouching in front of a computer. A home office designed well will not only lessen your discomforts but will also provide you with the best environment for concentration and relaxation.

The Best Home Office Setup Ideas 2020

There are no set guidelines for how to create a home workplace. Your home office may look something like an IKEA office or a beanbag in the yard.

These ideas are available regardless of your preferences.

1. You don't need to be indoors

It doesn't necessarily have to be inside your home office. "Garden offices" allow you to maintain the highest separation between your personal and professional life. This can be a fully furnished home office with a kitchen and bathroom.

Although it may cost more to set up a garden office, it can provide the ideal location for a beautiful home office structure.

2. Decors can be used to liven up your workday

Your home office space should be built solely for the purpose of achieving quality work. It doesn't necessarily mean that you shouldn't add some decoration to your home office. A few pictures, houseplants, and other devices can brighten up dull spaces. If you have a space that encourages positive thinking, you'll be able to accomplish more.

Some decorations are more business-oriented. To emphasize the importance and value of time, some productivity professionals like to keep their clocks at hand.

3. Stay Clear of Clutter and Keep Your Necessities Close by

Are you prone to running around the house looking for paper or pens, or just to grab a drink? For drinks, you should consider adding a small refrigerator to your office. You can store all the things you need in your home office cabinets and racks. These cabinets also provide a place to put your mess. Studies show that visual minimalism increases productivity.

4. Remember Your Lighting

Except for the rare case where you are averse to being surrounded with bright sunlight just to reminisce about your cubicle, other than that, lighting your home office is essential. You shouldn't be sitting directly in front of a windowsill. However, it can distract you from your work. Proper lighting, rest and proper lighting are two key ingredients to increasing productivity.

Consider placing your desk near a window to get natural light during work hours. For any reason that you may need light during the night, it is a good idea to get light bulbs that replicate natural lighting.

5. Investing In the Right Technology Equipment Increases Productivity

A lot of people work at home and do their majority of their work via a computer. You should invest in a high-quality mechanical keyboard that will accelerate your typing speed and a comfortable mouse that reduces hand and wrist strain.

6. Ergonomics are Essential for Productivity and Health.

Poor ergonomics not only reduce productivity but can also lead to serious problems like back pain or carpal tunnel.

Here are some suggestions for ergonomics in the home office:

Set the computer's height so that your monitor is at your eye level. This setting is a great way to reduce eye fatigue and neck cramps.

* Make sure that your keyboard is set at a level where your lower arms are parallel to the ground. This helps reduce the chance of wrist pains from prolonged work hours.

High quality work chairs available

Quality work chairs are worth the investment. A noisy, uncomfortable chair can be distracting and even cause permanent discomfort.

Sitting at a desk is not advisable. Sitting for prolonged periods of time is bad for your health. But a standing desk can help to alleviate this problem.

There are many factors that will determine the ideal home office setup. Different people have different needs and preferences. You can still use these suggestions to set up your home office space, no matter how simple or expensive.

Chapter 3: How To Work From Home And Stay Productive

If you worry about how your productivity may decline when you work from home, this chapter will explain the y strategies you can employ to get more done and be more productive.

When it comes to the productivity of remote workers, there is a common misconception. This is totally false.

However, remote work can improve productivity and performance. It is a known fact that remote workers tend to spend about 1.3 more days on productive tasks than their on-site counterparts. Remote workers can make it difficult to maintain a healthy balance between work and family life.

Unexpected changes in the workplace have meant that few companies had the time or resources to build their capabilities and strengthen their culture. Workers are now working from home, which can lead to isolation. They can do this from their basements, kitchen tables, or homes.

These seven strategies can help you to deal with all the obstacles that you might face as a remote worker.

You should create a work schedule that you stick to.

A work schedule is a great way to increase productivity at home and to get more work done. Similar to what you do at work. This may seem like a simple task, but once you have so much time to handle it all, things can get complicated.

A majority of remote employees work from home and have a schedule similar to your regular 9-to-5. The bottom line is that you should be responsible for every second of your workday if you feel completely in control.

You won't be able to keep up the deadline if you don't have a schedule.

You will know when you are at your most productive. You could be more productive in morning, but not able do any logical work at night.

For 2-3 weeks, experiment with different times to determine what works for you. You can track your performance every day to find the time that works best for you.

Take breaks

No matter what your mind tells you, it is essential to schedule consistent breaks. You can break your work time into 3 hour blocks, then take a 1 hour break. You may be allowed to take the entire day off, provided your organization allows.

Even if it's not necessary, you can still get the rest you need to keep you energized. Burnt out can also lead to a decrease in productivity. People don't want to have to do the same thing over and over again if they are trying to get a job done faster.

Breaks give us a boost of energy, help us stay focused, and allow us to be more creative. This is why most people think their best ideas first thing in the day, or after long periods or meditation.

This is the catch: you won't fall behind at work because you spend 2 days on your TV binging your favorite show. Indolence at work for too long will lead to a lazy lifestyle. Poor time management will always produce terrible results.

Prioritize your time

People working remotely often have poor time management skills. Very few people are skilled at managing their time and organizing their activities.

You may feel that you are never able to make your daily tasks a priority. Here are some tips:

Begin by starting with the tasks that are not enjoyable.

If you are too tired, move the administrative tasks to afternoon. Your creative juices will be at their lowest. You should not spend your energy on unnecessary tasks that do not contribute to your primary goals. Don't do this. It will sap you of the energy necessary to accomplish the most important tasks.

Give this tip a try to increase your productivity. You should keep it going for a few days. It is not something you will like because it is difficult to keep it up, but it is highly effective and it can be applied immediately.

Video calls should be handled professionally

You'll be amazed at the amount of distractions that can happen in just one meeting. As team members spend so much of their time trying help each other, meetings can lead to a lot wasted time.

Zoom and other video calling applications have solved this problem. They allow you to put any image you want in the background. It's similar to a screen that gives you the option of using a background photo.

Keep your desk organized

It is a great way to increase productivity. A cluttered desk can make people miserable. Some prefer a minimalist computer desk. There are also those who like to place a variety of pictures, notes and candles on their desks. Both of these situations are not caused by clutter. We stress more because we feel like they don't belong in their right place.

Here are some helpful tips to clear clutter from your desk.

1. You can stop moving documents to other files after you have placed them in a clear order

2. Do not buy souvenirs or decorative items that aren't needed and you might never use. Fake flowers and figurines are a great way to make a statement.

3. According to the purpose of your desktop, divide it into 2-3 segments. This will enable you to determine where to find it.

4. Keep an eye on your images and documents regularly to ensure that they are up-to-date.

5. To make it easy to clean up your workspace, try to keep it as empty as possible.

Keep your personal and professional life separate

This is a major challenge for those who work from home. This is a real challenge because you cannot do this work from home without separating the two. You may have encountered two problems that every home-based worker faces:

Your family thinks that you are available for a 2-hour chat, or shopping.

You work overtime every day, even though you may not be aware.

The first problem is easy to solve:

Have a private place to work in your home

Some people go so far as to use their basement as a workspace, in an effort not to get distracted at home. If you find that this is feasible, it's perfectly acceptable. Put a sign in your office door whenever you're working to let your children and family know that you are available for them when they need you.

This is a common situation. The reason people work remotely is more productive is that they are free from the distractions of an office environment where a colleague can come by and interrupt you. You and your computer are all that matters at home. Once you have eliminated all time-wasters, you'll be so immersed in work that it is difficult to remember the time.

Clear your mind.

It is nearly impossible to disconnect your mind from work-related concerns when you are having a casual conversation with family members or cooking dinner. The human mind is an open place and it can be difficult to control.

Instead, it is important to get rid of any physical work prompts. This will allow you to be more productive working remotely.

* Turn off the computer

* When it is your closing time, you can turn off email notifications

* Lock your house office.

Learn how digital apps work

There will be days when you aren't in the mood for work or days when you may be unusually slow. This isn't a huge deal. We all feel it at some time.

How can you be productive when such days come along?

Digital tools can be your friend. Digital tools allow you to dictate your articles even if you're distracted by other tasks. Digital tools allow you to do your job faster. Digital tools help you eliminate stress from administrative tasks so that you can focus on what is important to your creativity and skills.

It's not difficult to remain productive when working at home. These proven strategies can help you increase your productivity. It's okay to take a short break. However, you should stick to your schedule and avoid any actions that might cause you delay your tasks.

Chapter 4: Essential Tools To Remote Work

You will have to adapt to working from home. For you to stay connected and do the job efficiently, you will need more apps than ever before. Here are some tips and tricks to help you stay connected.

1. Tools for team communication

Why do you need tools to facilitate team communication?

Communication is crucial, no matter where you work. Because you don't have to meet up with your colleagues on the street or stop by their desks for chit-chat, it is important that you find another method of communicating every day.

It's a good idea to send them email. Email can be time-consuming, especially when you are having a lengthy conversation with more than one person.

You can make a mistake that could ruin your entire conversation. When working from home, it's essential to create an application for continued discussions with multiple individuals.

Slack is a great tool for team communication.

2. Tools for presentations or meetings

Why are tools important for presentations and meetings

Virtual meetings, remote presentations, and video calls are all common ways to think of remote working. This is not true. These are crucial components of working online, especially when it comes to clients and teams. A reliable and effective tool to conduct video calls is key to remote working.

Zoom is a powerful remote collaboration tool that can be used for video-conferencing. It's also very easy to use, even for beginners. Zoom is the leading teleconferencing software in the market today. It offers standard features such as video meetings and presentations, screen sharing, chat, and touch-ups.

Skype, Join.me GoToMeeting and Blue Jeans are some other tools available for presentations and meetings.

3. Tools for project managing

Although it is hard to keep on top of your own tasks, it can be quite difficult to coordinate the tasks and responsibilities for your team remotely. It's possible. There are tons productivity tools for remote workers that can help you and the team stay on task, regardless of where you're working. These tools come in different formats to suit different industries, sizes, and working styles. AirTable and Asana are all useful tools for project management.

4. Time management tools

Some people incorrectly believed that working remotely meant not being time conscious. This is false. You will find that time management is much more important when working remotely than in an office environment. No matter whether you are working as an independent contractor or as part of a team, time management tools will allow you to maintain your productivity.

Google Calendar is a wonderful time management tool. You can keep your schedules clean and coordinate with your clients and team members for work sessions. It can help you avoid scheduling conflicts while ensuring you have time to do work and enjoy your leisure.

RescueTime and Toggl can also be useful time management tools.

5. Tools for writing and editing

It can sometimes seem that words have lost relevance due to the vast amount of video and image content available online. While working remotely is a great way to learn writing and editing skills, it can be difficult to master them. You will still have to make phone calls and video conferences, but much of your communication will happen via email and chat. Even if you don't have a tech-based job your work may be administrative. This means that your work will involve a lot more writing, editing, and revising marketing messages and other documents.

Grammarly is a powerful writing and editing tool. You can simplify your writing tasks and make your writing more efficient. Grammarly can assist you with all forms of writing: emails, lessons or website copy. You can use it on your mobile or desktop device to complete all of your writing tasks.

You can also look at other editing and writing tools such as TextExpander or Evernote.

6. File Sharing Tools

For efficient teamwork, it is crucial to have an effective way to share information. Secure file sharing tools, regardless of whether you are at work or at home are crucial to the survival your company and organization.

Google Drive is a web-based service that allows users to store, share and collaborate on digital documents. It's a valuable tool, especially if you make use of other Google products like Gmail and Docs. Google Drive allows you to save and manage documents from other computers (e.g., Apple and Microsoft).

Other good file sharing programs are available, such as SpiderOak and OneDrive.

Chapter 5: How To Find The Right Remote Job

This section contains tips and information that will guide you in your search for a remote job. This chapter covers everything you need, from the industries most likely to have remote jobs to the best sites to get a remote job. It also provides valuable tips on how to prepare a portfolio for remote positions as well how to prepare yourself to interview for remote positions.

The current market is flooded with remote and work from-home jobs. This is a significant improvement on the situation in recent history. It can be confusing to know where and how to search for these jobs. However, before you decide to go all-in and get a job, make sure it's something you truly want. Otherwise you may find out that remote working is not what you are looking for. Answer this question.

Are remote jobs right for me?

Are you really ready for remote work?

Remote work is possible for some professions. Remote working is possible in some of these areas: customer service and marketing, as well as remote technology jobs. Some executive roles include consulting, freelancing, and consulting.

Some jobs are not suitable to be remote. One example is a construction worker who cannot work remotely. A surgeon, however, can.

There are many remote options available, so there's no need to work for one company.

You can work part-time for different clients and take on multiple jobs. You may prefer to work with one company.

Consider the one that best suits your needs. Perhaps you only require part-time work because of the money. Maybe you need to acquire different skills in various roles. Maybe you just want to do contract work for a few weeks and then go on vacation.

Types Of Remote Jobs

I will show you a list ten of the best remote jobs. These jobs will suit many skill levels and experiences. It doesn't matter if you're a techie or a 100-word per minute writer. You'll find something you love.

Translator

Translators are the first job that can be done remotely. The internet is making the world smaller. This means that businesses have to find ways to reach people in other countries. A translator can help. A translator can perform a number of tasks for businesses, such as testing a website, translating documents, or proofreading. You will need to speak at least two languages. Fluency in more languages is an advantage. If you are interested in looking for translator jobs, visit Fiverr or Upwork. These places are used by companies when they need to translate documents and do the job.

Designer

Designers are highly valued by remote companies. Designers are able to do everything from graphic design to designing Shopify themes to UX/UI design, all while working within a structure. However, design does require some design knowledge. The good news is that there are lots of resources to help you learn design knowledge. The great thing about remote jobs in design is that they will continue to be in demand in the future. Companies will still require websites that are attractive and functional. For this reason, talented designers will be sought.

Our remote work environment is a great place to find jobs in design. Remote working is a great way to find work, development, or marketing opportunities.

Copywriting

Copywriters are professional writers for companies. They can help businesses write everything, including the language used on the homepage, product pages, and emails used for email marketing. A good copywriter does not require you to be a top-notch writer. You can also be persuasive if your sales experience is a plus. Then, look for remote copywriting opportunities. These opportunities can be found on flex jobs. Flex jobs can be filled in many different roles. However, it is also a place where larger companies look to hire remote talents. Flex jobs is a great place to bookmark whether you are looking to work for a start up or a larger company remotely.

Social Media Manager

Social media manager is next up on our short list of remote jobs. You might be looking for a remote job that leverages your scrolling experience on Instagram, Facebook, or tick tock. A social media manager could be right for you.

You can easily manage your social media accounts from your own home. You must communicate with the brand for which you are working and any freelancers who help you to put together your social media content plans. A social media manager job that is remote requires you to have previous experience on social media platforms. You can still learn these skills if you work for a small company.

Digital Marketer

Digital marketing is the next remote career on our wish list. This could be the job for you if your skills include selling ice to polar bears. Online marketer is the umbrella term that covers all of the marketing disciplines within this umbrella. This could include affiliate marketing, search engines optimization, search engine advertising, and remote marketing. Remote marketing does not require any special equipment. Marketing is about the ability and use of online tools to keep track of your marketing trends. Remote OK is a great resource for remote marketing jobs. Remote ok is an enormous job board, with many remote jobs, including marketing. Remote OK also provides statistics on top remote jobs and top companies.

Virtual Assistants

Virtual assistant might be a good remote job. Virtual assistants can make life easier for others by doing the essential but tedious tasks. Virtual assistants are used by many dropshippers as well as entrepreneurs to accomplish their tasks. Virtual assistants could help with customer service emails, scheduling, fulfilling orders and managing calendars. Being a virtual assistant requires you to be extremely organized. You also need to communicate well and have a 100% trust rating. Part-time and full-time virtual assistant jobs are great. You can launch a business, make some extra income and become a virtual assistant by applying to UpWork.

Customer Support Specialists

Customer service specialists may be the right job for you if you love working remotely and are good at communicating with customers. This job requires that you can use chat or phone software to answer customer queries and solve problems. You must be an excellent communicator to succeed in this position. You must be able and quick to understand the product or service that your support is providing. Virtual assistant jobs offer customer support as part-time and full-time options. This allows you to easily add it on to another job.

Transcriber

The next job is that of a transcriber. This is a remote position and is great for someone who is an excellent listener as well as a quick typer. Transcribers use audio files to create written texts. Many professions rely on transcribers. These include medical professionals, podcasters, and many others. Being a transcriber requires the ability to quickly write while listening and not miss any details. It sounds easy but it can be difficult. This is why it's such a popular remote job, and many companies will continue to use transcribers for the next few months.

Finally, if there is one type of remote job that you can do online, it's development. No matter what level of engineer you are, whether you are a full-stack or app developer, it doesn't really matter. Online work is possible and many remote companies offer remote jobs. Remote jobs don't require that you take a salary cut.

Your skills are in high demand and you can negotiate with remote companies. If you don't want to become a developer, find resources that can help you learn this skill and then contact a remote company to get some real-world experience.

Chapter 6: These Are The Best Websites To Find Remote Work

We work remotely

We Work Remotely might be the largest remote job board. It attracts more than 250,000 people every month who are looking for remote jobs or posting them. There are various jobs, such as copywriting and programming, or marketing.

FlexJobs

FlexJobs, another great website for remote jobs, is also available. This website is very user-friendly. You can also find executive and professional jobs. The website offers 50 job options, so you can be confident that you will find the right job for you.

Motivate

This website not only provides a job search portal but also offers a weekly newsletter for telecommuters. There are more than 100.000 individuals searching for their dream jobs every month. The vast majority of them find it. This platform is for everyone interested in jobs in HR, Marketing, Customer Support, Engineering, Sales, and Education.

Dribbble

Dribbble is an online platform for designers. It was founded in 2009 and has been very popular among design professionals. Over 40,000 companies trust Dribble when looking for remote employees.

UpWork

Upwork is a very popular platform for freelancers. Although you won't receive a contract offer through the platform, you can always find job opportunities that are right for you. UpWork requires you to register, get approved and then you can begin searching for jobs. You can also send your proposals.

Themuse

Themuse offers many remote jobs. You'll need time to search for something you like.

Angellist

Angellist is the perfect place for you if you are looking to work for a startup. Angellist has many opportunities to help you get your remote work.

Freelancer.com

Freelancer.com lets you connect with over 31761,297 employers as well as freelancers around the globe. You will find a variety of jobs from programming, writing, engineering, and even law.

Fiverr

Fiverr allows you to start your freelancing career with services starting from $5

Toptal

Are you interested to learn more about finance? Toptal is committed in finding the best financial advisors and offers great jobs in reputable organisations. Toptal collaborates with Zendesk (Pfizer), Airbnb, Zendesk, and many other companies. You won't want to miss this opportunity!

Working Nomads

Working Nomads offers a simple interface to make navigation easy. These are the most highly-sought-after positions on the site: administrators, developers, advertisers experts, designers and managers. Also, you can find work in education, health law, and education.

Solid Gigs

Solid Gigs is a time-saving tool that helps you maximise your time. Each week, they find the best jobs for you through email. Additionally, they have many templates, scripts and interviews that you can use when applying for a job, negotiating with your employer, or any other issue.

CloudPeeps

CloudPeeps can be a great place to learn if you have a lot of knowledge about marketing and copywriting. You will find good jobs with a commensurate salary if your standards are high.

College Recruiter

Finding a job can sometimes be difficult if you are still in school and have not graduated yet. College Recruiter helps students to find part-time, freelancing opportunities that offer them the opportunity to earn money, build their portfolios and gain valuable work experience.

ServiceScape

ServiceScape completed more than 259000 jobs. This platform is ideal for anyone who is interested in working alongside start-ups. This site also offers freelancing opportunities for writing, editing, design, and translation.

Freelance Writing

This platform was launched in 1997, and has remained the best platform for freelance authors ever since. The platform is completely free to use with an intuitive interface. It also has many job openings.

Envatostudio

Envatostudio has the perfect place for you if you are an illustrator or design expert. You can explore different categories such as interface design, animation, audio, graphics, and many more.

SkipTheDrive

This website is very easy-to-use and offers jobs in any sector you choose. You don't need to register for the service.

The Creative Loft

This platform is perfect for photographers who are passionate about photography and can edit well. It offers part-time or full-time work, so even if your student status is not yet confirmed, you can still make some extra money by working here.

Rent a coder

You can find thousands in programming jobs by renting a coder. Employers and employees can be matched based upon their experience. You may also be able to get long-term work.

PowerToFly

PowerToFly, founded in 2004, brings together women from different parts the world in the technology field. Its goal: To help women find rewarding tech jobs in organisations that embrace diversity and inclusion.

Work-From-Home-Friendly Firms

Aside from the above-mentioned sites, there are many other regular companies that offer various types of telecommuting positions. These range from entry-level jobs to advanced degrees.

The following organizations can be a great place where you start your search for work-at-home opportunities that will pay your bills.

Amazon.com Inc.

Amazon.com Inc. employs 750,000 people worldwide. A significant portion of these employees work remotely. Only a tiny percentage of Amazon employees work at the headquarter in Washington. The company had 30,000 available positions for remote workers in September 2019. Amazon has many representatives scattered all over the globe, so people who don't work at the headquarters of Amazon do not feel neglected. Amazon offers many different work-at home opportunities, from global account manager jobs to customer service jobs.

Dell Inc.

Dell's corporate headquarters in Round Rock is located in Texas. Dell offers both work-at–home and flexible jobs. These include working at its headquarters as well working remotely. It is also known for its employee-friendly benefits like compacted workweeks. The company also offers work from home opportunities in a variety of fields that require different degrees and expertise.

Humana Inc.

Humana is the third-largest national health coverage organization. It employs nearly 49,000 workers both on-site, and remote. The remote workers work in every aspect, from sales management that requires exceptional interpersonal skills but does not require any specific education to the position for a physical therapist that requires additional years of college coursework.

Aetna Inc.

Aetna Inc. a Fortune 500 medical-care organization allows employees to telecommute once they have been employed for at least one year. You can also work remotely as a customer service agent, administrator, or frontline nurse. To keep employees informed about what's going on at work and to communicate with coworkers, they have access to a range of technological tools.

American Express Co.

American Express offers a variety of work-at home, part-time, and full-time jobs. These jobs include business development manager (a job that usually requires several year's experience or an MBA), and part-time online customer service representative positions.

American Express supports a balanced work-life and personal development of its employees.

Kaplan

Kaplan's areas are professional training, K-12, and online higher education. Kaplan also offers test preparation to help students write the standardized tests required for College admission. The most sought after work-from-home position is that of a tutor. This job is not office-based but requires the tutor to travel for students. A tutor can earn between $10 and $20 an hour, and depending on student demand and tutor availability, may work up to 40 hours per week. Kaplan mentors are candidates who have taken the GRE, SAT or SAT and performed well.

Salesforce.com Inc.

Forbes named Salesforce.com, (CRM), one world's most innovating companies. Fortune magazine also listed it as one top 100 workplaces. A significant portion of the company's 49,000 employees work at home. Work from home opportunities for the organization required a lot of experience. Salesforce's entry-level candidates should seek out sales jobs, such as a field account executive, in order to work from home.

Automatic Data Processing

Automatic Data Processing provides global outsourcing solutions and payroll processing for businesses. Most of the work-at home opportunities are in sales and customer services. Therefore, entry-level candidates have the opportunity to get recruited. Programming and application development offer higher pay, but require special technological skills.

Xerox Corp.

Xerox offers remote job opportunities and flexible work arrangements to its employees. Executive recruitment requires sales experience and a bachelor's degree. Part time call center jobs are available with no education requirements. Project Management requires many years of experience.

Avoid these Scams

Working from home has seen a significant improvement over the "make money stuffing bags" promotion. Be careful if you want to make some extra money while staying at home.

You can do background checks on any potential employer that works from home. It is important to ensure you only deal with a reliable and established company. If there is no proof that the company has a physical location and renders services or sells products, you should not deal with them. Track the contact number. Many fraudsters pretend to be agents or working directly for reputable organisations.

As with any regular job, there should be an applicant and possibly an interview. Everybody who wants to hire someone will want to talk with them. You shouldn't spend money on your own to get hired. You should not pay any upfront fees, purchase starter kits, or make any financial obligations to a remote employment opportunity. This is most likely a scam. However, you will need to have an internet connection that is fast, reliable, and steady.

Chapter 7: How To Prepare For Remote Interviews

The rise of computerized workplaces has made remote interviewing more popular. Remote interviewing is becoming increasingly popular as the workplace shifts to more remote work. Even if an older worker, you might still be subject to remote interviews at some point.

Some people believe that remote interviews can be just as effective as face-to–face interviews. Remote interviewing presents unique challenges.

This chapter will provide guidance on how to prepare for remote interviews. When you are moving into unfamiliar waters, it is important to be prepared. The following tips will help make sure you are prepared for remote interviews.

Recover before you go

Being well rested before a remote interview is essential for our health. You won't be disappointed by the benefits of getting enough sleep. Your memory and ability to concentrate will improve. You'll also feel more creative.

It is important to get sufficient sleep before you travel for remote interviews. This will allow you to give your best performance.

It is not necessary to sleep as you will not be traveling to the interview. It is important to sleep at night for either 30 minutes or one hour so your body can adjust to the best possible level.

Do your research for the interview

It's crucial that you prepare for your interview. You may be asked by your interviewer to perform tasks or take a test on the computer as part of your interview, because technology has made it possible to do so many things.

You should familiarize yourself with the organization as well as the job descriptions before you go to the interview. You don't have to spend endless hours researching, but you must be prepared for any remote interview.

It's possible to be asked why your position is important. You will benefit from knowing what the position involves and what you can expect to do. This will enable you to impress potential employers.

Dress for the Occasion

Dressing professionally for remote interviews cannot be stressed enough. The company expects that your appearance is professional. They don't expect you to arrive at the interview wearing your bedroom clothes. Dress appropriately for the Interview.

Do you want to make sure your equipment is working properly?

Remote interviews are carried out using technological tools. Ensure that you have the right tools and applications to use during the interview.

You can test the tool before you go to interview to ensure it is functioning properly. Many of these tools offer the ability to simulate real life situations. You should check that the microphone is working, that the camera is working, and that your internet connection works.

The worst scenario is that you log on to your interview applications just five minutes before the meeting. You will run into many problems and this will cause you to be late and upset.

Common Remote Interview Question

Let's talk about some of the questions that may be asked during a job interview. Although you may be focusing on remote jobs or work from home opportunities, this doesn't mean you won't be asked some of the same questions when you meet with potential employers.

Here are some questions you should ask when looking for a remote job.

Why would you choose to work at home?

This question is bound to come up in a live interview. Here are some steps to help you prepare to answer effectively.

First, make a checklist. Do some soul-searching and brainstorming. Then, be honest with your self. Are you truly interested in working remotely? You should be more specific about your reasons for wanting a remote job. What is the most out of control in your current job? Do you want to work at your peak productivity time? Do you want more time with your kids?

Next, explore the benefits telecommuting can bring to businesses. Did your employer know that it is possible for them to save money, increase turnover, or increase productivity by allowing their employees remote work? Knowing why remote work is a good option for businesses will help you to map your motivations to these benefits. Flexible schedules lead to more productivity and fewer sick days. It's something both you as well as your potential employer can appreciate. This mutual benefit can be used as a starting point to explain why you want a home-based job.

Remote employers want to hear from you why working remotely is a good idea, but they also want your ideas on what you can do. If you answer their question with benefits, it will impress the interviewers. During the virtual interview, it is important to keep your focus on the employer and remain positive. It is important not to suggest that you wish to work remotely in order to have more time for your passion projects or because of your inability to work well with others. Employers may be turned off by these statements.

Did you ever work remotely before?

This is another question that may be asked during interviews. Yes if you've ever been a remote worker. Even if the work was only part-time for a few weeks, that answer would be "yes."

What is your preferred work style?

This question is a bit more difficult than it sounds. It's still not as simple as, "Why would you like to work in this company?" Perhaps you have ever worked remotely.

Most likely you already know your personality type. If you're a natural extrovert you will be the one who is eager to go to work every day, whether it's to speak with people or just to check out the latest news. If you're an introvert, it's likely that you enjoy working in your own time and are more comfortable doing things alone.

But, working remotely or in teams is not the same thing. We must learn to work together no matter what our personalities are. You need to be careful when answering this question. It's not enough to say "Yes, I like working independent" or "Yes, I like working with others." The employer might want to know if your personality is extrovert/introvert. Give it some thought. It is important that you fully answer this question, because employers, even remote ones want to know if your personality is extrovert/introvert.

How can I stay organized and on track with deadlines?

Sometimes working remotely means you can work late at night, because your computer's always there. It is important to have a set schedule at home. How do I stay organized and on track with deadlines? This is all about your home office setup. Do you have piles of papers or folders that are neatly organized and placed in the right places? There are many time management tools you can use to stay organized. These are important things to consider so you don't get lost when your potential employer asks.

How would you describe your communication style.

This is not my favorite question. But think about the communication style you have. But just because we are professionals doesn't mean that we want to communicate the same way. I always ask clients what their communication style was when I meet them for the first time. One client asked me this one time. It was while I was working in the office. The client wanted me to meet with her face to face every meeting. She didn't want me e-mailing her, nor did she want me Skype with her. She only wanted me to be there in person. Although this was not my preferred communication method, it was what she requested. You can make a difference by paying attention to your communication style. This will ensure that conflict is minimized by getting to know your colleagues and your managers.

What are your experiences with digital communication tools and how did they help you?

Working remotely means that you can live anywhere you want. All meetings are conducted virtually. You should have had experience using digital communication platforms. Even if your experience isn't professional, most people have communicated electronically, even via Facebook. Do not just say that you've held meetings on Facebook. Think about the way you might answer that question. Don't assume that you don't know how to use these tools, or that you haven't attended professional meetings. Even if it wasn't, set up an appointment online with them to practice. It's important.

Do you feel capable of working with minimal supervision

This is another tricky question. As an adult, this question is not a problem. But, it is possible that the employer asks this question to suggest that the job requires a lot self-motivation. This is a good idea. Is it necessary to have a lot more supervision? Although it's not important to show that you can work on your own, it's a valuable skill.

These are just a couple of questions you need to think about before meeting with your potential manager.

Chapter 8: Sources For Homeworking Jobs

It's exciting to notice that homeworking jobs have become more varied. They don't just apply to multilevel marketing agencies like Avon. The rise in technology has led to many companies offering homeworking jobs. This is also because these businesses want to reduce costs and save more.

Some examples of job sources that can be used for homeworking include:

Health And Medical Sector

This sector has many companies that offer homeworking work. UnitedHealth Group is a top-rated company, along with Humana Group, Covance. Aetna. Paraxel. Forest Laboratories, and many other. Some of the homeworking jobs they offer include phone-based and computer-based ones, and they include sales representatives, business-intelligence managers, medical writers, patient-case advocates, and patient-education advocates. They also have revenue-integrity and account managers as well as actuarial consultants and case managers. Registered nurse case managers, clinical nurse managers, and other remote job opportunities have been offered by these companies in recent years.

Education

Many people will not accept the idea of working from home in education. The advent of online learning has resulted in the introduction work-from-home jobs in this field. Tutor.com, InstaEDU or Connections Academy are some of the online educational companies. These companies have helped to create part-time positions and freelance positions, such as parent mentors or curriculum writers, and SAT tutors. Other jobs that can be done as homeworkers include student-services coordinators, parent mentors, science teachers, and student-services coordinators. VIPKID in China is an online education company that provides students with access to American education. Additionally, the online-teaching staff at this company can benefit from a flexible, homeworking program.

This field offers excellent opportunities for people who speak multiple languages fluently. Appen, a company that coordinates communications between clients from different parts of the globe, is one example of this niche. Asurion offers excellent customer support in different languages, and is the best choice for helping with product insurance plans for electronics companies. These companies need translators as well as interpreters.

Government

It is impossible to associate Government agencies with innovative or unusual personnel policies. However, there are some flexible types of work being adopted by some national-level, state and local institutions. The federal government is a pioneer in encouraging telecommuting, as has the state. In fact, the federal Government is more proactive than private companies in promoting telecommuting policies.

In addition, the federal government teaches employees the benefits to working remotely. Research shows that only one federal employee works from home at any particular time during the year. The federal government's agencies include the department in control of Transportation, the agency in charge in agriculture, as well as the department that is in charge in the interior. Homeworkers include affairs officers, security experts, economic advisers, emergency service planners and security specialists.

Engineering and technology

The most common type of homeworking is technology, which is a surprising fact. The creation of engineering and virtual office has been a result of technology. These offices offer their services on a per project basis. RedHat (SAP), First Data, RedHat (IBM), and IBM are just some of the top-rated companies in this sector. These companies also offer high-tech sales jobs for homeworking. Remote workers can find jobs as project managers, technical writers and software developers.

Chapter 9: Friendly Companies Offer Work From Home Jobs

Many telecommuting jobs are available at most legit businesses, even those that are not part of the Fortune 500. These include jobs that require an experienced individual, someone with advanced degrees, as well as those who have entry-level positions. For a top-rated job as a homeworker, here are some options:

AMZN

Amazon.com Inc. employed more than 500,000 people, many of them from different parts. The majority of these employees work from their homes. There are only a few employees that work in the headquarters of the company, which is located in Washington. The company has extended its workforce to every part of the globe. They all love their jobs and don't want to be replaced.

Dell Inc.

Dell is another high-rated firm that offers home-based jobs. Its headquarters in Austin, Texas, is also a top-rated one. Dell offers flexibility, such as remote working and flexible hours. It is well-known for its worker-friendly perks such as compressed workweeks. Dell offers several types of homeworking jobs. However, the education requirements and experience levels vary between each other. These positions can range from outside sales to marketing support and tech support.

Humana Inc.

Human Inc. is a large health insurance company with over 50,000 employees. They work both from their homes and on the job. They perform all tasks from sales management, which requires basic knowledge, to physical therapy, which is a job that requires post-college coursework.

Aetna Inc.

After you've been with Aetna Inc. for a year, you can work from your home. Telecommuting jobs offered by this company include customer service representatives, supervisors, and frontline nursing staff. The company offers telecommuting positions that allow you to work from your home and access all of the technology available. This allows you to stay informed of the latest developments in the company and keep in touch with your coworkers.

American Express Co.

American Express Co. is another top-rated company offering friendly homeworking positions. The company provides a range of homeworking jobs, including part-time, full-time, contract and full-time. You will find a wide range of assignments that can be done as homework, such part-time customer service and business development. Americal Express is also a highly rated company that offers great work-life and personal growth opportunities for its employees.

Kaplan

Kaplan refers the tutoring firm that helps students prepare to take the standardized test required for admission to graduate schools. This tutoring company has the most requested tutoring job. While the tutoring job requires little or no office time, it may require you to travel to meet with your students.

Kaplan pays its tutors at least $20 an hour. They can also work as many hours as they like per week, though this all depends on how much demand there is and their availability. The firm hires only high-performing candidates on standardized exams.

Salesforce.com Inc

Fortune Magazine placed Salesforce.com in the top-rated companies to be a worker for. Forbes also named Saleforce.com one of the top innovative firms worldwide. It has over 25,000 home-based employees, making it one of the most highly rated companies. The company requires years of experience to be able to telecommute. Work from home jobs for entry-level workers include field sales accounts executives and field sales reps.

Automatic Data Processing

Automatic Data Processing provides outsourcing and payroll solutions to businesses around the globe. Customer service and sales services are its most popular home-based jobs. This indicates that there are high chances for an entry level candidate to land a job. Another work from home task offered by the firm is software development and applications. However, this requires special technology skills.

IBM

IBM offers telecommuting jobs for candidates who are located in the US or elsewhere around the world. International Business Machines also offers a perfect opportunity for freelancers who are looking for work as a homeworker. It offers contract work for researchers, software developers, and chemical engineers. The company also pays by postal mail. A majority of IBM employees are able to work from home. One of the best things about freelance jobs, is that most are looking for a unique skill.

Xerox Corp

Xerox Corp. is also a good option if looking for a work-from-home opportunity. This is not the only reason Xerox Corp is so popular with employees. It offers flexible scheduling and allows for many people to work on-site. The company provides a variety of work from home opportunities, including project management. This job requires several years of experience, as well as a call center role, which doesn't require specialized education. The company offers executive recruiting as a telecommuting job. This requires sales experience, as well a bachelor's.

Chapter 10: The Best Homeworking Jobs

There are many homeworking jobs that can be done by corporate employees. Most people who work as freelancers are employed by companies. They can choose to set up their own businesses. Many companies are now targeting independent contractors in order to fill multiple roles. The ideal option for people who are organized, have time and can manage several projects simultaneously is homeworking. The majority of enterprises turn freelance assignments into small businesses and even employ some of these workers.

Below are examples of highly-rated homeworking positions. Some positions require specialist expertise and training. Others don't.

Virtual Assistant

A virtual assistant can be compared to an off-site secretary. A company will likely spend more on a traditional secretary than they do on a virtual assistant. Small companies do not require a full-time secretary. They communicate with their bosses via Slack and chat.

This employee is unique because they are able to handle all tasks that traditional secretary can. These tasks include data entry. Calling clients, managing social networks, creating company documents, scheduling appointments, responding to various emails, and booking. Virtual assistants can also do these tasks for a fraction of the cost. These job requirements require a minimum of office experience and exceptional communication skills.

Translators

Translations are a necessity for international companies. This is where translators can help with transcribing and translating conference conversations, documents, and other files. This field is in high demand and there are many positions that can be done from home.

Customer Service Representatives

Today, many organizations, big and small, are outsourcing customer support tasks to agents who work remotely. Customers are more likely to have issues communicating with agents who don't speak English fluently or have accents.

Therefore, the US is a preferred destination for American customer service representatives.

Most customer service jobs involve inbound calling, which is where they assist people with their account information and orders. Other jobs may involve outbound call. Some others have a set work time, while companies pay per hour. These individuals must have great communication and interpersonal skills. When recruiting customer service reps, most companies will do background checks. Companies often hire traditional customer service agents to answer questions from customers. They can also be available via social media or the website.

Data Entry and Transcription

Although there are many jobs, data entry and transcription tasks require similar skills. Data entry is the act of filling out a spreadsheet with data and figures. You will be working with a customer management software to enter inventory items, catalogue items and payroll data.

A home-based worker will create transcription documents by using audio files. This work is intended for companies that need a podcast or conference calls, workshops, meetings docs, or other similar services. The company will typically provide the software and content management system required to complete the task. When hiring workers, the company will look for detail-oriented individuals and people who can type well.

Tutor

Because of the rise of online education, online instructors have become a hot commodity. A virtual school can be described as a whole. These schools focus on offering high school-level education programs as well as college-level learning programs. You will also be able to find faculty at these schools from anywhere in the world.

Yes, teaching qualifications are required for most online teaching positions. However, online tutoring isn't. However, before hiring tutors, the company will verify their education. If you are able to tutor advanced subjects, such as calculus or physics online, you will be paid more per hour. A chance to score standardized tests online is also possible. A college degree or teaching background may be required for scoring tasks.

Beware Of These Scams

While homeworking began with money-making ads, it is now a completely different story. Yet, studies still show that scammers are present in 57 percent of legitimate gigs. You should be extra cautious if your goal is to work from home.

It is essential to take your time and get more information about the homeworking employer prior to you agree to work with them. Work with a reputable company. An established company is the best. It must provide proof that it sells a specific product and also have a physical location. Make sure to verify the contact information and make sure it works. You will be surprised at the number of con artists claiming to work for corporations.

For the best job, you must apply for it and be interviewed. An employer that is trustworthy and willing to talk with you must be the best. You shouldn't be paid to do homework. If you're asked to pay for a homeworking job, it should be considered a scam. To have reliable internet access, you must be willing to make a small investment. You don't need one to do this.

Chapter 11: What You Need To Know About Homeworking Jobs

Similar to office work, homeworking comes with its own merits. It is still the best choice, despite the fact that the benefits of doing homework are greater than the drawbacks. You should not forget these crucial tips to make the most of homeworking. These are:

1. You determine your success or failure

The best part about working remotely is that you can set your own work hours. This is a clear indication that your success or failure is at your fingertips. Your ability to focus, hustle, or interact with other people is entirely up to you. What you produce and how you receive it is entirely up to you. There is no reason to feel guilty about your workday, especially if it's at your home office.

You will still be the boss, even if you work remotely as an assistant. Be prepared to be alone and face the same challenges every day, if your home office is chosen.

2. Follow Deadlines

Prepare to deal with those who don't see homeworking as work. It is important to set your hours and stay consistent. Do not let others interrupt your work schedule. Others will see you only as an employee and will interfere with your schedule. This will negatively affect your ability to complete your tasks.

It is important to recognize that there are many distractions in your home life. These interruptions could cause delays in important projects and interfere with your work schedule. These include emergencies such as those involving children, pets, accidents, vendor calls or power outages. These are just a few of the many personal disruptions that may occur.

Family members need to understand that it is impossible for them to move when they are working. You should also let your family know that you cannot chat while on the phone. As a parent it can sometimes be hard to set limits. You can also have a positive impact on your children's career choices and future attitudes by working harder in the field you love.

3. It's impossible for you to leave the office

Working from home is preferred by many people for its flexibility and efficiency. People also prefer to work from home because they have fewer hours. Doing homework allows you to complete your tasks without interruptions from staff meetings or emails. Sometimes it is difficult to treat your house as an office. Sometimes it can be hard to pretend you're working from your home.

Poor time management is the main reason that most home-based workers work more hours. Other workers will find themselves working on weekends or at night because they don't follow their schedule.

Research shows that many home-based employees work five hours a days instead of eight. This doesn't mean that they don't accomplish their daily tasks. Hours are calculated as billable hours. This means that companies charge hourly for the time they use, but not for the time they use to do non-compensated tasks.

4. It might be hard to save

While you might think working from home will save money because it doesn't cost anything for attire, lunches, or commuting, that's not the truth. There are many other expenses that will be incurred. Business services, mobile phones, laptops, internet service, software, webhosting, printers, business cards and cell phones are all required to establish an office. All of these are important things to consider before working from home.

For the cost of the internet and your home office, be prepared to deduct 50% of your mortgage. You cannot claim return credits or deductions for homeworking. However, you can deduct any work expenses that are valid. This is only available if the work is related to your work. You cannot deduct all the costs of the internet service your spouse, your children and/or spouse use for purposes not related to work. Only deduct that portion which is intended primarily for employment-related issues. For office utilities and telephone bills, as well as office supplies, do the exact same.

Independent contractors will need to pay payroll taxes. This is the expensed that most workers cover. You won't see any significant reductions in your tax bills if you do homework.

Chapter 12: Homeworking: How To Make The Most Of It

Around four million people work from their homes, according to research. Managers of different companies claim that home-based employees perform better than their office-employees.

Home-based workers have a higher efficiency and are less stressed. This positive record results in lower absenteeism as well as higher morale. Doing homework is an excellent choice for your environment, organization, and employees.

Work from home has its problems. These can include job and professional difficulties, to physical and psychological problems. How can you be more productive and still stay healthy? Here's how to find out:

1. Get a Schedule

A majority of people prefer to work at home because they are able to create their own schedules. It allows you to work whenever you want. It takes only a few minutes to complete the task and then you can spend the time doing what pleases you.

You must be careful not to waste your day. To ensure that every day is worthwhile, you should develop a schedule that works for you.

Working from home is best when you eat your meals at a specific time of day. A good rule of thumb is to always start your work and stop completely at the exact same time every day.

An excellent schedule will allow you to know when you need to be at work and when it is time to go to a break, attend meetings, or call someone.

2. Take a picture of your work and batch it

Although a work plan can help you achieve your daily goals, it's also important to schedule your daily tasks. Doing this will help you do more work in a short time.

Research has shown that multitasking makes us less productive. Batching work remains the best way to maximize your productivity and be more successful.

If you can group what you need, it will be easier to get the job done right the first time. By preparing your meals for the entire week on Monday you will be able to save even more time.

Another option is to dedicate a month to planning everything you will share on your social media platforms over the following months. You'll quickly realize that this is a wonderful way to save your time and money.

3. Get ready for the morning

Most people find it simple to get out of bed and head straight to their home office. While it is a very productive step, there are some things you can do to make it even better.

If you don't put on clothes before going to work, it helps you focus on the day ahead. In addition to this, you are more likely to be productive if your clothes are real. Don't work in your sweatpants. According to research, our success and thought levels are directly affected by the clothes we wear.

4. Always Stop at a Specific Time

Your schedule can only be kept if you begin the project on time and end it at the agreed time. If you work at home, you are more likely to be lazy and feel like your time is less valuable. If you work from home, this can also happen.

If you are determined to stick to your daily work schedule, you will be more productive and more successful. If you struggle to stop working, it's likely that you will quit your job.

By choosing to share a happy moment, you're more likely to interrupt work. This is also true if you enjoy dinner with family members or friends. If you work eight hours a days, you're not productive. By working for only eight hours a day, you allow your body and mind to recharge and relax.

5. You can set aside some days for meetings or other tasks

Your daily schedule can only be met if you make time for calls and other tasks that are not related to your work day. By doing this, your mind will be ready for whatever day comes.

Aside from this, setting aside some days to call and meet with people will reduce interruptions so you can focus on the daily tasks. You can also set aside days for meetings or other tasks to give yourself the peace of mind that you require.

6. Track all Hours

It is essential to track all of your hours so you can see how much time you are spending. It is true that you will be responsible for tracking the hours spent on the assigned project. However, it is also important to track the time you spend elsewhere.

This will allow you to see the wasteful things you do, and help you focus on what you can do to change. This could be anything from chatting on social media to web surfing, or even just browsing the internet.

It will also help you track your hours and identify important tasks. There are many top-notch activities you can do during these hours, including cooking and interacting with family members.

To be more productive, start to track your time so you can become more successful.

7. Make a boundary between your 'Home' space and your 'Work' space

People prefer to work at home because it allows them to work from anywhere. Many people work from their homes and move around only to their living spaces, kitchen tables, offices, and bedrooms. Others do them all, and they end up more productive and highly successful.

The same way you can easily walk into an office at work, your home office will also have to shift your mindset.

This shift is vital because it provides a lot of benefits for the home worker's brain. This shift is also helpful in indicating to family members that the home worker is working as per their usual work schedule. You will be able to sleep at night without being disturbed by your family.

8. Decluttering Your Physical Space

It is essential to keep your workspace clean. It's crucial to avoid being distracted by the clutter around you. This, along with the time and money savings, can make a tidy office a great asset.

Organization is a major cause of company losses. Research shows that this loss can be attributed to a lack in productivity and distractions.

In addition to this, a messy workspace increases the likelihood of viruses being transmitted via keyboards or smartphones. If this happens, you are likely to get sicker days.

Cleaning your workspace should be done at least once per week. You can do it in as little as ten minutes.

9. You can purchase ergonomic, comfortable furniture for your office.

This is not a good idea. However, you can't do it any other way. Face it, if you're doing work that demands sitting for long periods of time and a computer.

It's a good idea to use a standing desk or to improvise on a high table or counter. Also, it is essential to take regular breaks and stand up for short walks. You should also make walking meetings or calls.

You should also consider buying office furniture that is comfortable for your posture. The furniture must be properly fitted to the body.

10. The right atmosphere

Because everyone works differently in offices, they are often referred to as controversial. You should also create this environment when working remotely. It is important to set the perfect mood, light the perfect candle and have a clean workspace.

If you are an introvert, or someone who struggles to work in noisy environments, it is better to work in peace. Avoid coffee shops and open offices as these could distract you from your work.

All people are not created equal. Some individuals will be able to work while listening to YouTube videos or watching TV. Others may have trouble with online applications. However, you shouldn't attempt these if it is not possible.

It is vital to find something you enjoy so you can feel comfortable at work.

11. Avoid Social Media

Research shows that many people spend more time on social media than they need to in a single day. Although it is perfectly acceptable to do this, it leads to a decrease in productivity for most employees, which ultimately affects the company.

When it comes to wasting time, most people are the worst. Although most will go on Facebook or Twitter for updates, many end up spending an hour answering others' questions or responding in some other posts.

Since they can feel lonely, social media platforms are great for those who work from home. It is easy to get away and connect with your friends from the comfort of your own home. But be aware that social media can quickly take over your work time.

Home-based workers need to establish timers through extensions and applications. This allows them to keep on track and helps avoid clicking on URLs from social media.

12. Check Your Emails at Specific Times

Also, checking email can be a time-waster. Your inbox will keep sending you new notifications, which can cause discomfort and make it impossible to work effectively.

Being a home-based worker can make you more productive, but it isn't always possible. You may not always have access to the internet and be available at all times. If you want to increase your productivity and earn more, then this is the way to go.

Set a time and place when you will check all your emails. It is important to set up notifications so you don't get disturbed every time someone sends you an email.

Sometimes, it's a good idea set an autoresponder so that you don't allow distractions or to control you. For example, you could set a time to respond to your email at 10 a.m. 2, 3 p.m., and 5 pm.

13. Set expectations for working hours

Homework can be difficult because it requires you to communicate expectations and guidelines with your family members, housemates, and neighbors.

One example is that your partner may love to discuss their day at home. If you are still working on your daily projects, however, this could distract you.

To ensure you're happy and not being interrupted, it is important to set expectations. This highlights the importance of setting a clear time for you to quit your job and the work schedule.

You might decide to notify your family members when you aren't using lights. To avoid interruptions, you can switch the lights on and off when you're not working or on a call.

14. Useful Ways to Procrastinate

Relaxing and recharging your mind can make you more productive. We can waste so much time procrastinating by using inefficient methods.

Sometimes you'll plan to do something useful in a short amount of time and end up doing the contrary. A 5-minute YouTube Video may show you how to organize your home office. However, it could end up showing you a 20 minute video about the best places around the globe.

It is important to find productive ways of procrastinating, which will allow you to achieve both your short-term goal and long-term one.

Some people take a short break to go to the kitchen and cook. Others will take a short walk inside their homes. Other people will use this time for brainstorming ideas and creating an outline of a specific article.

It is vital to be able to think while you work. These breaks should not be wasted.

15. Please Contact Us If You Need Assistance As A Parent

Parents who work from their home face a unique challenge when it comes to managing their children. You will be less productive if your work is interrupted by taking care of your children.

As with any office work, it's important to be able work comfortably without being interrupted by your kids for the designated time. It can be difficult to simultaneously take care of your kids and work remotely. People expect parents to take care both of their children and work. While it can be hard to find the right balance, working remotely is possible.

This is where you should seek out help. You need it to be able to accomplish your daily tasks, even though you work remotely. Some parents work out this solution by ensuring that one of their children works later than the other.

Some families find it more enjoyable to send their children to part time daycare facilities, so that they can be productive without interruptions.

If any of the above options do not work for you, it's important to tell your employer. Your employer will then assist you in finding the best solution.

16. All Notifications Can Be Disabled

For homework, distractions come in the form of notifications. They are addictive and irresistible. We need to do everything we can to make sure they're off. Slack is one example of such notifications.

Today's world is filled with apps that want to interrupt your attention. It's important that you turn off any notifications from apps while you work and only check them during breaks. This will help you be more productive. Do not allow these notifications to distract you from your work.

17. Make sure you use the most appropriate tools to stay on track

It is important to invest in the tools that can make your job easier for freelancers or entrepreneurs.

Apart from investing in trade-specific products, it is vital to invest in affordable ways for automation tasks. This will ensure that you don't need help.

Calendly is a Google Calendar plugin that can help you schedule your calls. When the person assigned to work completes this form, they'll receive an email along with a link that will allow them to schedule the best time to chat via the calendar.

Calendly also offers the possibility to increase productivity as you can only schedule your calls for certain days.

You can automate different tasks, such as proposals, invoicing, and project management.

18. Headphones with Noise Cancelling Technology

It is great when you can work without being interrupted by audio distractions.

You need these headphones to reduce noise. These headphones are useful for both working in your home or while traveling.

With noise-canceling headsets, distractions will be minimized so you can remain focused on your day-to-day project.

19. Online Community

A major disadvantage to homeworking is that you miss the in-person community and your co-workers.

While dogs and cats can make great work friends, they won't be able to provide stimulating discussions that help you move past hurdles as you work, create new tasks, or come up with innovative ideas.

Online communities will provide the perfect solution for the absence of an in-person element. This site will give you access to many online communities including Slack groups, LinkedIn communities, Facebook community, and Twitter communities. These communities make it easy for you to ask questions, share successes, complain, laugh, etc.

It is essential to find the best online communities for your needs. You'll be able to look and feel exactly like other members of the crew.

20. Leave Your House

You can work anywhere you like with homeworking. It is possible to work at coffee shops, where all you need is a snack or a drink.

A co-working space is another option. Another great option is to go to a friend's house to work. You can also opt to finish your day outside on one the restaurant patios, if it isn't too hot.

It is essential to change work places in order to spark new ideas. You can also make your work more productive by changing your workplace.

21. Keep Family and Friends Informed About Your Work

In cases where you do all the work yourself, homework can leave you feeling lonely.

Keep your family updated about your work so they know what is important and can avoid interrupting. You can also make your family invest in what you do.

If your family members and friends are able to understand what you do, it will motivate you more and make you more productive.

22. Break the Habit At The Very Most

Yes, it is essential to set up a work schedule. But, it's important to break it apart every once in awhile. It is possible to decide to take your cat on a short walk to the closest park. You also have the option of attending either the morning or nightly coffee networking meeting.

Additionally, you can take a few hours off work to visit an art museum in your locality. You get flexibility with your work schedules, which is an outstanding benefit of homeworking. If you can break away from your routine at least once a week, you'll be more productive.

23. Rule 20-20-20

You can prevent eye strain by using the 20-20-20 principle. This is an easy way to avoid eyestrain, which occurs when you stare at your computer screen multiple hours per day.

After staring at your screen for 20 minutes, give yourself a 20-second break.

It is important to use your time by focusing on an object 20 feet away. Doing this will allow you to relax your eyes.

Blue-light blocking glasses, or the following rule, will make it easy to keep your eyes healthy.

FREELANCE WRITER

Freelancing allows you to work remotely at your own pace and is the most cost-effective, efficient, and convenient way to get started. The freelance writer can be employed as a part-time employee or in entrepreneurship. The usual hourly rate for freelance writing is $50, although some projects may take several days or even months. You can charge by the hour. It can be as high as $50 an hour or as low as $100 depending on the project. It doesn't need any special software. You don't need any special software. Because it's flexible, you can start part time and increase your income as the job progresses. You can grow and advance from the beginner level by doing research about the job, becoming familiar with writing tools and writing tools, blogging, organization skills, growing your confidence, practicing writing, building a portfolio of work, and then pitching for jobs.

Freelancer sites such as Fiverr, Freelancer or Upwork let you register. These sites offer many services. It is possible to land a job right away if you register at one of these websites. Consider displaying your work online, and applying for gigs. Once you have done that, decide how to get paid. It's important to be prepared for anything, including paying your taxes, buying your healthcare, funding your retirement, or managing your income stream and expenses. Freelancer.com can be a good resource.

Growth

* You will need $500 to begin, but if there is a computer and high speed internet, you can start with $500.

* It takes two months to create, and you must take courses to improve your skills.

* You can get a raise in your hourly rate from $50 to 100

Here are some helpful links

* You can see videos related the job in YouTube

* You may start with Fiverr.com

* After some time you can apply for Udemy Training Courses and Freelancer.com.

Pros and cons for a freelance writer

Pros

* It can be flexible

* You have the option to work with many clients or you can turn down any that don't work for you.

* You can make so many!

* Your success and advancement are yours.

Cons

* You might need to work for free

* It can take over your life if allowed.

* You are also responsible if you fail

* Your clients might not communicate with you.

SOCIAL MEDIA MANAGER

As a social manager, you can earn money if your time is spent on social media. Social media managers manage the social media accounts of celebrities and business owners. They earn money for the clients and businesses that they work with. They can charge per hour, monthly, or per project. A social media manager is responsible for planning and scheduling content across different social media platforms.

Start by training. Select a platform where you have experience, such as Facebook or Instagram. You can then create your website or build your own social media platforms. Learn how to build your portfolio and understand your target client. Apply for social media manager positions to expand your client base. From home, you can make as much as $25. Fiverr.com offers a useful link.

Growth

You will need $500 to begin, but if there is a computer and high speed internet access, you can start with $500.

* It will take at least two months to build, and you'll need courses to continue your education.

* You can get a raise in your hourly rate from $25 to 50 dollars

Here are some helpful links

* You can see videos related the job in YouTube

* You may start with Fiverr.com

* You may apply for Udemy training programs after some time. Then, you can apply in Flexjobs.com

What are the pros and cons for a social media manager?

Pros

* You will be paid on your social media platforms

* Your work has a positive influence and the potential to go viral

* You can request feedback regarding your progress

* Your work could be very original

Cons

* Work can be put under pressure if you have to deal with major emergencies or new information

* Keep learning and growing to improve your performance.

* An error can go viral

CALL-CENTER REPRESENTATIVE

A representative from the call center answers client calls and can provide assistance or redirect calls as required. Customer satisfaction is assured by the call center representative. The software used to update client information and place orders can be updated. Training is provided to ensure that the representative stays current. Organization procedures are followed to determine if a client's query can or cannot be resolved. A high school diploma or equivalent is required for a call centre representative.

Call center representatives may work from their homes or an office. Companies may use your expertise to meet their business needs. The job could last from one to ten hours per week, depending upon the agreement made with your client. As little as $9 to $15 per an hour is possible. A registered telephone, high speed internet service, and excellent communication skills are all you need to start. There will be a background check after you are offered the position. Upwork.com is an excellent resource.

Growth

* You will need $400 to begin, but if there is a dedicated phone, computer, and high-speed broadband internet you can start with much less.

* This will take about two months to develop and you will need courses to help you learn more as you move up the ranks.

* Increase your hourly rate from $9 to $15.

Here are some helpful links

* You can see videos related the job in YouTube

* Upwork.com can help you get started

* You can then apply to Flexjobs.com

A Call-Center Representative's Pros and Cones

Pros

* You have very flexible scheduling

* You may be trained to perform the job

* It's very rewarding work

Cons

* You must be totally free from distractions

* You can't trust anyone to provide support

* You can get a call center job at a different level

PHARMACY MANAGER

Many large insurance companies will hire pharmacists who can work remotely. Consulting in the area of the specialty you are interested can let you work from your own home. The job may require you to do clinical research, reviewing or writing, as well consulting. The duration of the job can vary depending on whether it is hourly or monthly. It allows you more flexibility in your work hours and can be a time saver. First, you'll need your pharmacist certification, a laptop and good internet service. This job is rapidly changing as everyone requires a health specialist. Based on the project, you could earn anywhere from $30 to $40 an hour. Fiverr.com offers a helpful link.

Growth

* $300 is the minimum amount you will need to start, but if there are computers and high-speed internet access, you can start with less.

It will take at least two months to create, and you will need courses to help you learn more as you move up the ranks.

* Your hourly rate can go up from $30 to $45

Here are some helpful links

* You can see videos related the job in YouTube

* You may start with Fiverr.com

* Apply after some time for training courses in Lecturio. Then, go to Flexjobs.com.

A Pharmacy Manager's Pros and Cones

Pros

* A thorough understanding of the job

* It pays well and has many benefits

Cons

* There is not enough training for certain tasks

* It is hard to manage people

AFFILIATE MATERIAL

Affiliate marketing is about making money. And you can do it from your bed or anywhere else you are comfortable. Affiliate marketing is where a virtual store pays you a commission on sales and traffic from your referrals. Affiliate marketing allows you to recommend products or services to your followers via your blog or email list. Your followers can then purchase the product and/or service by using your affiliate hyperlink. In return, you receive a commission.

All you need to get started in affiliate marketing is a laptop and high speed internet service. You can also create a blog or website about your niche and promote affiliate products and/or services. Select products and services relevant to your niche. An affiliate network can help you do this. Affiliate networks are businesses that link merchants with affiliate marketers so they can make more profit. Affiliate networks offer more information about how the products or services are selling. You can use this information to increase affiliate marketing profits. Create quality content that is profitable for affiliate marketing. Include your affiliate link in the content. Then, convert visitors to customers through your site. Use your email list to reach growth. Email marketing remains the best way to make more passive income. A customer can earn $50 and you have a 2% chance of converting. This job can take up to 24 hours. It is revenue-generating. Fiverr.com can be a good resource.

Growth

* Start with $500, but with a computer and high speed internet you can work with less.

It will take at least two months to build, and you'll need courses to help you learn more as you move up the ranks.

* You can get a raise in your hourly rate from $50 to 100

Here are some helpful links

* You can see videos related the job in YouTube

* You may start with Fiverr.com

* Apply in Flexjobs.com for Udemy-approved training courses.

Pros and cons of Affiliate Marketing

Pros

* You can still generate income while you sleep

* Low investment costs

It doesn't mean you have to leave your job.

It is easy to use and flexible

* It makes you independent

Cons

* Earn based on your performance

* Customer service problems can be problematic

* Your competitors can't be controlled

* There is no guarantee you will generate any revenue

* It's impossible to establish a solid customer base

* It's possible for affiliate links to be hijacked

ANIMATOR

The animator creates animations for television and other media. They may specialize in one of the media or a certain area, such as background designs, characters or scenery. They use computer software for their work. They work together with their clients, producers, or other animators to create prototypes. To be able to complete a task, animators must have more than artistic talent. They need to have creative skills, time management skills as well as listening and communicative skills. The rise in technology has led to an increase in the demand for animators skilled at computer graphics, especially for smartphones. Depending on the deadlines, animators may work for hours, weekends, or holidays. They could also work 50 hours per week. Working as an animator from home can pay you between $50 and $100 per hour. Fiverr.com offers a helpful link.

Growth

* You will need $500 to begin, but if there is a computer and high speed internet, you can start with $500.

* This will take about two months to complete and you will need courses to help you learn more as you move up the ranks.

* You can get a raise in your hourly rate from $50 to 150

Here are some helpful links

* You can see videos related the job in YouTube

* You may start with Fiverr.com

* After some time, you can apply for Udemy training programs and apply in Flexjobs.com

Pros and cons of an animator

Pros

* You will be compensated for your creativity

* There is an underlying sense of freedom and independence

* You save money on your commute

* Enhances quality life

* The ability to adjust work schedules if necessary

Cons

* You work long hours

* You work all day to meet the deadline

* Invading clients can lead to stress and unstable pay

BAKER/CHEF/CATERER

If you are deciding to provide home-based catering, then you should be able to concentrate on one type of food, or event. Is it possible to deliver and cook at your clients' home? Or can you cater from home? Once you have decided everything, it's time to order your equipment. You need cooking utensils and pans for your business and not your kitchen. You can now start cooking and set up your home-based catering services.

Choose the type of catering business you wish to open. You will need to apply for your license, permit, and liability coverage. Now you are ready to start. It is possible to make between $10 and $15 an hour. Remote.io is a good resource.

Growth

* You will need $500 to begin, but if there is a computer and high speed internet, you can start with significantly less.

* It will take about a month to build, and you will need to take courses as you move up the ranks.

* You can get a raise in your hourly rate from $10 to 25 dollars

Here are some helpful links

* You can see videos related the job in YouTube

* Remote.io is possible

* Apply after a while for Skillshare-approved training and then submit your application to Flexjobs.com

Pros and cons of a Baker/Chef/Caterer

Pros

* Making money from what you love is a great way to improve your health.

* Existence of a good marketplace for good foods

* Being able to unleash your creativity

* Ability to sell products online

Cons

* Keep your catering equipment separate from your kitchen gear

* A separate kitchen is needed for your business.

* Earn money only when your business is sold

* Ensuring your compliance with any environmental regulations

BOOKKEEPER

You can make a living as a bookkeeper and enjoy the flexibility and freedom you seek. This job requires no special equipment. You only need a computer, an internet connection, and bookkeeping software. While the experience may be valuable, certification is not required. A bookkeeping job requires accuracy and meticulous attention to details. A general ledger is maintained, payroll reports are filed, inventory reports are managed, petty cash is monitored, project budgets are tracked, and inventory counts are recorded.

Hourly rates for a Bookkeeper range between $20 and $50, depending on the complexity of the job. Business vary on how many hours they require. Bookkeeping jobs can also be found on sites like Acuity and Bookminders.com. Get your tools, create your website, and market your business using social media platforms.

Growth

* Start with $500, but with a computer and high speed internet you can work with less.

* It takes two months to create, and you must take courses to continue your education.

* You can get a raise in your hourly rate from $20 to 50 dollars

Here are some helpful links

* You can see videos related the job in YouTube

* Upwork.com can help you get started

* After some time, you can apply for Udemy training programs and apply to Flexjobs.com

A Bookkeeper's Pros and Cones

Pros

* There are very few startup costs

* You can work virtually

*You can increase your target market

* There are no necessary pieces of training

Cons

* There could be liability issues

* It would be best to take important steps to ensure the security of client data.

* Accounting software may be very expensive to purchase

CHILDCAREGIVER

Child caregivers can be very rewarding. You could open your own daycare in your home. It can be very profitable. You can only make as much money from this business depending on where and how many children can you care for with a license. It is a great opportunity to make a lot of money while also helping young children. You can help your children's lives by being a parent but still own your business. You also don't have to pay someone else for daycare. You could earn up to $45 per workday and as much as $1200 per working week. The duration of the job depends on what agreement you make with your client.

No special certificate or degree is required to start your own business. To get started, you will need a daycare license. Your ability to communicate with your clients is key to your job's growth. A strong relationship will bring more children. An unlikely link can be helpful.io

Growth

*You will need $900 to begin, but if there is a computer and high speed internet, you can start with less.

* It takes two months to create, and you must take courses to continue your education.

* Your pay can be increased by as much as $40 to $65 per calendar day.

Here are some helpful links

* You can see videos related the job in YouTube

* Remote.io is possible

* After some time, you can apply to Flexjobs.com

Pros and cons of Child Caregiver

Pros

* While you are running your business, it is possible to look after your children.

* Your schedule follows normal business hours

* You can positively impact the education of young kids

* There should not be any shortage of potential customers

Cons

* Startup costs could be costly

* It is beneficial to have insurance to protect your family and your kids

* If you take care of many children, you might need to use a lot more space in your house.

CLINICAL-RESEARCH COORDINATOR

It is the responsibility of a clinical coordinator to facilitate and coordinate clinical research' daily activities. They also need to help with trial administration including financial, compliance, staff members, and other important matters. A clinical research coordinator can make up to $40 per day working from home. However, the average salary in Canada and USA for this position is $46000. While the typical work environment for clinical research coordinators is in a lab environment, they can also work from home. You'll need a computer with high-speed Internet access and clinical research equipment. Start by getting health-related information from the client. upwork.com can be a helpful link.

Growth

*You will need $600 to begin, but if there is a computer and high speed internet access, you can start with less.

* It will take at least two months to build, and you'll need courses to help you learn more as you move up the ranks.

* You can get a raise in your salary from $40 to 100 per day.

Here are some helpful links

* You can see videos related the job in YouTube

* Upwork.com can help you get started

* Once you have completed your training, you can apply to Medvarsity and Flexjobs.com.

What are the pros and cons about a Clinical Research Coordinator?

Pros

* You can get started after you have earned a bachelor's Degree

* A job that makes sure medicines are safe

* You can do a lot of different job duties and still have a lot to do.

Cons

* It can be stressful

* You spend your time working on paperwork or sitting at a computer.

CONSULTING

A consultant is someone who is authoritative and knowledgeable about a topic. Due to your experience and knowledge, clients and companies are more likely to pay for you. Independent consultants can work independently and from home. This makes it easy to secure contracts in a highly competitive freelance marketplace. If you want to be a home-based consultant you must first identify your niche, obtain the certifications or licenses, determine your goals, research your target market and get your office space. You also need to fix your fees, market your business, market it, and determine whether you need outsource any tasks. Begin as a beginner to build lasting relationships with your clients. As you progress, you will become a consultant. The project and your experience will impact the hourly rate. You'll need a computer and license. Fiverr.com offers a helpful link.

Growth

* $500 is the minimum amount you should have to start, but if there are computers and high-speed internet access, you can start with significantly less.

It will take about a month to build, and you'll need courses to help you learn more as your skills improve.

* You have the option to increase your hourly wage from $20 to 100 dollars

Here are some helpful links

* You can see videos related the job in YouTube

* You may start with Fiverr.com

* After some time, you can apply for Udemy training programs and apply in Flexjobs.com

What are the pros and cons to consulting?

Pros

* This job comes with a high hourly income

* Keeps your skills sharp for future employment opportunities

* It is flexible

* By selecting your projects, it gives you the power to set your work schedule.

* The work may vary if you are working for different clients

Cons

* Building a business requires money and time.

* It may seem easy to collect money from clients, but it can be difficult for others.

* It doesn't guarantee a steady income.

COPYWRITING

A great way to make good money working from home is copywriting. While you don't have to have an advanced degree to do this job, it is possible to find a lot if one knows how. You don't necessarily need to be an expert in order to start. The pay gap can be a joke. Copywriting is part of sales writing. Companies may need it to create video scripts or white papers, videos, emails, whitepapers, presentations, product descriptions, white papers, whitepapers, white papers, white papers, and websites. Copywriters strive to convince clients and readers to purchase a product or take another sales-related action. Write an email or video script to convince readers to sign up for an on-line service. You will need to work for at least one year before you reach the $100000 mark. However, it is possible to make a small living while working on this job. Part-time work is possible, with 8 hours per semaine, but you can also go full-time to do copywriting jobs. You won't be able to wait long for a higher-paying position. Agency and corporate clients can hire a freelance copywriter. Earn $0.03 to $0.10 per Word at the beginning and increase your earnings as you work up. Make your job portfolio. You can then search for freelance jobs that match your skills and advertise your business on these sites. A computer, internet connection and a website are necessary. Earn $15 per hour. Fiverr.com offers a useful link.

Growth

* Start with $300, but you can get by with $300 if there is high-speed internet access and a computer.

* It takes one month to build, and you'll need courses to help you learn more as your skills improve.

* You can get a raise in your hourly rate from $15 to $40

Here are some helpful links

* You can see videos related the job in YouTube

* You may start with Fiverr.com

* After some time you can apply for Udemy Training Courses and Freelancer.com.

A Copywriting Review: The Pros and the Cons

Pros

* You can have many clients and job opportunities

* You can do many different jobs

* It is flexible

* Your creativity is yours

* You don't require a college degree, just your skills

Cons

It can cause fatigue

It creates solitude

* More creativity is required to match the preference of your client

STYLIST

It can be easy to start a salon from your home. You can set up your salon in your home. Before you distribute flyers or raid the beauty supply store shelves, it's important to understand the legal aspects. Make sure you have a designated space in the home. To grow a successful salon, and build client relationships, you must have a designated salon area in your home. Do not keep your head down, get serious clients. Be meticulous about keeping track of every purchase you make in your salon. It is important to be realistic about fixing prices. Don't underestimate your salon software. This can allow you to book appointments and manage your schedule. A computer, high speed internet service, salon tools, and salon software are essential. You earn $5.83/hour and can work hours, but it all depends on your clients and job schedule. Remote.io offers a helpful link.

Growth

*You will need $600 to begin, but if there is a computer and high speed internet access, you can start with less.

* It will take about a month to build, and you will need to take courses to improve your skills.

* Increase your hourly rate from $6 to $25

Here are some helpful links

* You can see videos related the job in YouTube

* You can begin in remote.io

* After some time you can apply to training courses in fashion stylist institution and apply to Flexjobs.com

Pros and cons of a Stylist

Pros

* You are able to have a personal interaction with clients

* You have excellent entrepreneurship opportunities

* You are satisfied by the job

Cons

* You must meet licensing requirements

* The wages are not as high.

* There are physical demands

SURVEY TAKER

Survey respondents get paid for providing honest answers to an online survey. Surveys are designed for an audience. Survey companies pay respondents based on the length and importance of the Survey. Some companies pay you only to answer questions. Your answers could be used to make the company money. The maximum price is $5-$200 in cash. Some surveys prefer points that can redeem for goods or cash. You can do surveys to get more points. Survey sites offer a way to earn good money. Some offer gift cards. You will see a rise in your growth if you join good survey sites such as Swagbucks or Prize Rebel. You will need a high-speed internet connection and a computer.

Growth

* You will need $500 to begin, but if there is a computer and high speed internet, you can start with less.

It will take at least two months to build, and you'll need courses to help you learn more as you move up the ranks.

* You have the option to increase your hourly rate from $55 to $200

Here are some helpful links

* You can see videos related the job in YouTube

* Freelancer.com can be your first job.

* You may apply for Udemy training courses and Survey Junkie after some time.

What are the pros and cons of taking surveys?

Pros

* They don't require a lot in terms of time

* You can complete surveys whenever you wish

* It's flexible, therefore you can multitask.

Cons

* You can also receive spam messages

* Being a survey taker can make it difficult to be rich.

* Not all surveys are open to you.

TAX PREPAR

Many organizations and businesses will need to prepare taxes. Tax preparation services can be a profitable business, even in difficult economic times. Keep up to date on annual changes. Manage and market your services for your customers and clients. A training course is available. Register your company as a tax preparation firm by filling out Preparer Tax Identification Number online. Set up a workspace in your own home with an internet connection, phone line, equipment, and space to store the hard copies of your clients. You can purchase tax preparation software, create business cards and market your services. Start with neighbors and friends. You should identify the customer for whom you are offering your service. Attract your target consumer to the business service. Show your business cards to your clients, explaining the benefits of using your service. It's possible to make between $10 and $15 an hour. You can also grow by taking on new courses for 72 hours each year. Remote.io provides a helpful link.

Growth

* You will need $500 to begin, but if there is a computer and high speed internet, you can start with $500.

* It will take about a month to build, and you will need to enroll in courses to keep up with your progress.

* You can get a raise in your hourly rate from $10 to $40

Here are some helpful links

* You can see videos related the job in YouTube

* You can begin in remote.io

* After some time, you can apply for Udemy training programs and apply in Flexjobs.com

Pros and cons of a Tax Preparer

Pros

* Time and money can be cut

* Income tax filings can be exempted from tax preparation fees

Cons

It might be more expensive than expected

* Be vigilant to avoid falling for scams

TELEPHONE NURSE

Patients can call or chat with their nurses via telephone. They assist their clients to decide whether they want to make an appointment or not with a doctor. They learn how to ask specific questions to help assess the case and then refer them to a healthcare practitioner. They can access the relevant records and health information of patients online. This gives them the ability to provide effective care for their patients remotely. Assisting doctors in reducing patient workload helps to reduce overcrowding in hospitals and decrease wait times. Dependent on their shifts, the telephone nurses may work 24 hours a days and 7 days a week.

Telephone nurses must be skilled communicators, able to think under pressure and have the ability to communicate well. Telephone nurses should be able to listen, assess and communicate with their patients the best treatment options. Telephone nurses do not have time to see patients. The job of a telephone nurse is not easy. They can make up to $41 per hour. All they need is a telephone and high-speed, internet service. This job is highly scalable, but can be very difficult to fill. This is a difficult link.io.

Growth

* You will need $500 to begin, but if there is a computer and high speed internet, you can start with $500.

* It takes three months to create, and you must take courses to continue your education.

* You can get a raise in your hourly rate from $41 to $75

Here are some helpful links

* You can see videos related the job in YouTube

* You can begin in remote.io

* After some time, you can apply for training courses at Lecturio.

What are the pros and cons for a telephone nurse?

Pros

* It can help you to save money

* It is convenient

It can increase patient engagement, communication, and communication

* It can expand accessibility

Cons

* There could be insurance issues

* The continuity of care may be decreased

* Technology barriers could exist

E-COMMERCE SHOP OWNER

The world is constantly changing and evolving into digitalization. This opens up a lot of opportunities for business people who are tech-savvy. Many people are quick to research products and make buying decisions. If you know what you are selling, you might be able make a great living working from home. It is possible to start an e-commerce store by buying the products and services you desire, setting up a dedicated workspace at home, creating an online store, or using social media channels, and marketing your business. This can be a difficult task, but if you take your time to follow these tips, your results could be amazing. Make sure you choose quality software and tools to grow your online business. You must have a blog that drives traffic to your website. Selling your products online is a key component of your long-term success.

You can use shopping ads for product sales because that's how you will target your customers. You need to make sure that your products are available through as many channels possible. Diversification strategies are key to growing an e-commerce company. You will see a faster growth rate if your ecommerce process is automated. You need to choose the right platform and carefully study it before making a commitment and investing in it. The tips I gave you, which depends on your niche, products and market structure, can help you make as much as $1000 per monthly. You will need internet access, software, and a computer. Fiverr.com offers a helpful link.

Growth

*You will need $800 to begin, but if there is a computer with high-speed Internet, then you can start with much less.

* It takes one month to build, and you'll need courses to help you learn more as your skills improve.

* You can get a raise in your hourly rate from $100 to 150

Here are some helpful links

* You can see videos related the job in YouTube

* You may start with Fiverr.com

* You may apply for Udemy training programs after some time. Then, you can apply for Flexjobs.com.

Pros and cons of being an E-Commerce Storeowner

Pros

* Low startup costs

* It is flexible

* He can earn money while he's sleeping

Cons

* There is intense competition

* It takes time and trust to build rapport with clients

* It could be experiencing technical issues

EVENT PLANNER

Event planning is about choreographing activities and people so that a show creates lasting memories. It could be a fund-raiser for charity, a meeting, corporate event, or tradeshow. Everyone wants events to run smoothly. Event planners will help to reduce stress and allow organizers to relax. It is possible to run your own event-planning business from home. This will allow you more freedom. It is not necessary to have a degree in event planning. Event planners can earn $12 to $75 an hour and vendor commissions. You'll need your computer, equipment, Internet access and an internet connection. To get started, you'll need to make a business proposal, pick a niche, create your website, market the event planning business via blogging and social networks, and invest in your company to learn more. While it might seem impossible, you can take the first step towards growing your business. Upwork.com can be a helpful resource.

Growth

* $500 is the minimum amount you should have to start, but if there are computers and high-speed internet access, you can start with even less.

* It will take at least two months to build, and you'll need courses to continue your education.

* Increase your hourly rate from $12 to 100

Here are some helpful links

* You can see videos related the job in YouTube

* Upwork.com can help you get started

* After some time, you can apply for Udemy training programs and apply in Flexjobs.com

There are pros and cons to planning an event

Pros

* Every event will leave you feeling satisfied

* Your clients will be more satisfied after every success

* You will have to create at work

* You will find interesting people in your contact list

Cons

* You may be able to manage other people's budgets

* There will so much responsibility

* Irregular long hours

* You might need to manage multiple events at once

GRANT WRITER

Non-profit agencies have to do a lot of grant writing. A grant writer collects documentation and meets the requirements of funding agencies to request funding. A grant writer should be an excellent and effective researcher who is able to locate the organization that can fund the agency. Also, they must know how to appeal for funding. Top-shelf research skills, superior organizational skills and exceptional computer skills are key to grant writers. Excellent and efficient writing skills are the essential talent for grant writers. It is not necessary to have a master's degree in grant writing. All you need for this job is an English degree. Although the impact of grants can seem hidden or subtle to outsiders, they are an integral part of the non-profit agency's functioning. A grant writer can also work remotely. A grant writer communicates with clients and donors, creates effective proposals, interprets grant guidelines, and ensures that the client's project is in line with requirements.

Internet access and a computer are all that's required. After you've completed these courses, you can get your grant-writing certification online. The American Grant Writing Association sponsors an internship program for grant writers.

How much grant writers can make will depend on how well they are able to handle their clients' workloads. Doing home-based grant work can help you earn up to $100 an hour. You can search online for grant writing jobs through social media or online job sites. Remote.io can be a helpful link.

Growth

* You will need $500 to begin, but if there is a computer and high speed internet, you can start with less.

It will take at least two months to create, and you will need courses to continue your education.

* You can get a raise in your hourly rate from $100 to $145

Here are some helpful links

* You can see videos related the job in YouTube

* You can also start from remote.io

* After some time, you can apply for Udemy training programs and apply in Flexjobs.com

Pros and Cons for Grant Writers

Pros

* You can work from anywhere, anytime as long as there is an internet connection and a good laptop.

* You have control over your time, schedule, and work at your own pace

* You can use your writing skills to help cause you care about

* Grant writing can bring in high-income opportunities

Cons

* You work solo all the time. Therefore, you are not socialized.

* There could be distractions

* You pay taxes and your benefits

* You might lack stability at work

GRAPHIC DESIGNER

Graphic design can also called communication design. Graphic designers create visual concepts either by hand or using computer software. They communicate ideas through visual art, which may include graphics, words, and images. Graphic designers' main goal is to make their clients well-known and recognized. To communicate identity and ideas, graphic designers employ a range of media. These media include logos, colors, billboards, images and print design. A graphic designer can be described as a visual-thinking communicator or problem solver. All graphic designers have the responsibility of creating specific creative outcomes or solving specific communication issues. Graphic design is increasingly being used in sales and marketing. Graphic designers must communicate effectively with clients, customers, and other designers to ensure their designs convey the desired message accurately.

Graphic designers who work remotely require access to a computer, high-speed internet, and graphic design software. Graphic designers work remotely and are responsible for managing all aspects of their businesses, including client relations, marketing, bookkeeping, invoicing, and billing. You will earn $100 an hour depending on your work ethic and commitment to the job. Your job duration and client deadlines are also important factors in this job's success. Freelancer.com is an excellent resource.

Growth

You will need $500 to begin, but if there is a computer and high speed internet access, you can start from less.

* It will take at least two months to build, and you'll need courses to help you learn more as you move up the ranks.

* You have the option to increase your hourly wage from $100 up to $150

Here are some helpful links

* You can see videos related the job in YouTube

* Freelancer.com can be your first job.

* After some time, you can apply for Udemy training programs and then apply in Flexjobs.com

Graphic Designing: The Pros and the Cons

Pros

* It offers creative freedom

* It allows you to work from anywhere using your laptop and internet access

* You can adjust your time to fit your lifestyle as long you deliver your work before the deadline

Cons

* You can work alone in relative isolation

* Pay can vary based on work flow

* You must be competitive and actively seek out projects

HANDMADE CRAFTTER

Handmade craft is a powerful way to emphasize the uniqueness, quality and individuality of a product. Handmade crafting means creating and designing work by hand. A handcrafted product is more valuable than one made by machine. It can be a way to earn money at home, doing what you enjoy and making a profit. It is possible to start by renting a workspace in your home. Then, get the supplies and a laptop with Internet access. This will allow you to make sales and find clients online. This business can bring in a fair amount of income depending on its niche. Make your website, market the business and look for customers. Each project can bring you between $15 and $40. Remote.io provides a helpful link.

Growth

* $500 is the minimum amount you should have to start, but if there are computers and high-speed internet access, you can start with $500.

* This process will take at least three months. You'll also need to take courses in order to continue your development.

* Projects can raise your salary by $15 to $55.

Here are some helpful links

* Watch related videos on YouTube about your job

* Remote.io is possible

* Apply in Flexjobs.com for Udemy-approved training courses.

There are pros and cons to being a handmade craftsperson

Pros

* You can make money doing what your heart desires from the comforts of your home

* You may have more ideas

* You create unique products

Cons

It can be stressful

* You cannot guarantee to have clients

* Profits are uncertain

INSTRUCTOR

An instructor can also refer to as a teacher. Teaching someone is the same thing as being an instructor. Instructors can either teach part-time, or full-time. It is convenient to start your teaching certificate in your home. Instructors are crucial. Instructors are in high demand across the U.S. To become a home-based educator, you will need to be a teacher certified. You can get teaching licenses and teach your clients. By studying online and practicing what you learned, you can quickly become certified as a teacher. It's easy to become an instructor once you have your bachelor's Degree and Certification. You can use your home to instruct your clients once you have received your certification. A computer, high-speed internet and a camera are all you need to become an effective instructor and earn at least $20 per hour. It is flexible work that allows you to take your time and relax. Upwork.com can be a helpful resource.

Growth

You'll need $500 to get started, but if there is high-speed internet and a computer you can start with less.

* This process will take at least two months. You'll also need to take courses to keep up with the latest developments.

* You have the option to increase your hourly wage from $20 to $40.

Here are some helpful links

* You can see videos related the job in YouTube

* Upwork.com can help you get started

* You can then apply to Flexjobs.com

The Pros and Cons Of Being an Instructor

Pros

* It is very simple

It is flexible and has no barriers to employment

It is convenient

* It allows interaction between client/instructor

Cons

* There are limits to the amount of interaction

* Internet connections may experience problems depending on the time of day

* Some schools don't count online teaching in their formal experience.

INTERNET SECURITY SPECIALIST

The average salary for an internet security specialist is $37 an hour and $77,000.15 per year. This job growth level is expected at 32%, creating up to 40000 new jobs in U.S. They are analytical, detail-oriented, and creative. It is important to determine the level of education needed to be a home-based Internet security specialist. A bachelor's is necessary to become a security specialist at home. Online learning is a great way to get management degrees and computer information systems. You'll need a computer, internet service with high speed and software to protect your internet. The equipment is easy to acquire, and you can then create your own website. You can also manage your business via social media platforms. This will help you get clients and customers. There are many resources available.

Growth

* Starting with $700 is a good starting point, but you can work with less if you have high-speed Internet and a computer.

* It will take at least two months to build, and you'll need courses to help you learn more as you move up the ranks.

* You have the option to increase your hourly wage from $30 to 100 dollars

Here are some helpful links

* You can see videos related the job in YouTube

* You can begin in remote.io

* After some time, you can apply for Udemy training programs and then apply to Flexjobs.com

Pros and cons of an Internet Security Specialist

Pros

* You can make a lot of money.

* You can find cyber jobs wherever you are.

* You have the potential of advancement

* A chance to learn and be creative

Cons

* It is costly to start

* Many jobs require demanding hours

* Some repetitive tasks may seem boring.

* To keep up to date, you must continue to learn.

ONLINE JUROR

Home-based online jurors can make additional money. It's possible to make more money online while also supervising the schoolwork of your children. Register on a reputable website for jury service and wait for your feedback. If you are successful, you'll be provided with a file you can use for a set period of work. Online jurors can help you to improve your skills, and make a living by offering paid trial income. It works the same as real courts. The difference is that online jurors present the cases to the online judges. Online jurors, who are well compensated for their services, then conduct the case proceeding. After an online hearing is completed effectively, the online juror will render a verdict. For the lawyers involved, the feedback provided by the online jury can be used to back up their arguments.

The best thing about being an online juror? You don't have to have specific skills. This makes it possible for anyone to earn more online. Online Verdict, Resolution Research, Virtual Jury are some of the reputable online juror websites that you can use to get started. Earn up to $100 per online trial session or $20 an hour. To start earning, you will need a computer that has internet access. You can also register at a reputable online jury site. Remote.io provides a useful link.

Growth

You will need to spend $400 to get started, but if there is high-speed Internet and a computer, you can do more.

* This process will take at least two months. As you move up the ranks, you'll need courses to help you learn more.

* You can get a raise in your hourly rate from $20 to $40

Here are some helpful links

* You can see videos related the job in YouTube

* You can begin in remote.io

* After some time, you can apply for Udemy training programs and apply to Flexjobs.com

Pros and cons for an Online Juror

Pros

* You can work at home

* This job doesn't require any special skills

* Save money

Cons

* You spend so many hours assisting cases

* You don't have to reach a conclusion based on facts

* You might give a wrong verdict

PET GROOMER

Pet grooming can be described as the caring and cleaning of your pet. A pet groomer can be someone who makes money grooming pets. Pet groomers take care of their pets to prevent health issues and maintain cleanliness. To become a home-based groomer, you need to take online grooming courses, have a dedicated telephone and a computer with high speed internet service. After that, your license will be issued. Based on your work experience and job, you can earn up to $10 per hour. A high school diploma is not required. All that's needed are your communication and interpersonal skills. Remote.io provides a link to help you.

Growth

*You will need $600 to begin, but if there is a computer and high speed internet access, you can start with significantly less.

* It will take at least two months to build, and you'll need courses to help you learn more as you move up the ranks.

* You can get a raise in your hourly rate from $10 to $40

Here are some helpful links

* You can see videos related the job in YouTube

* You can also start from remote.io

* Flexjobs.com allows you to apply after a period of time

What are the pros and cons about a pet groomer?

Pros

* You are able to set your own work schedule

* No formal schooling required

* This job is in great demand

It can be challenging, but it is doable

Cons

* Working with animals is frustrating and hard.

* Appointment is a requirement.

* You must be persistent in order to attract more clients

VIDEOGRAPHER

A videographer is responsible recording both small-scale productions and live events. They focus on small productions like documentaries, short films and legal depositions. Corporate videographers are employed by all kinds of companies. Their job is to create videos that help promote their products, services, or business. They also help to engage and sell people. They are creative and engage their audience with videos and their works.

On a temporary basis, home-based videographers can work on various projects. They can work for commercials, documentaries, birthday parties and other special events. They are independent and can pick and choose the type of work that they will do for clients. A videographer needs to be passionate about creating stories and messages via video and film. A computer with high-speed internet and video software is necessary to start making money as a home-based videographer. Advertise on media platforms, in your community or freelance sites like Fiverr to advertise for jobs. This job is challenging and you can earn up to $40/hour. Flexjobs.com is a helpful website.

Growth

* You will need $550 to begin, but if your computer is connected to high-speed Internet and you have access to a computer, then you can start with significantly less.

* It will take at least two months to build, and you'll need courses to continue your education.

* You can get a raise in your hourly rate from $40 to $60

Here are some helpful links

* You can see videos related the job in YouTube

* Upwork.com can help you get started

* You may apply for Udemy training programs after some time. Then, you can apply in Flexjobs.com

Pros and Con of a Videographer

Pros

* There are limitless possibilities

* There are flexible working hours

* You have enough potential for more money

Cons

* It is extremely stressful

* There are often payment issues

* Sometimes you could be exploited

PROGRAMMER

A programmer creates code for operating system and software applications. Programmers create code to transform the design of a software designer into instructions that a machine can follow. Run the program to identify errors and then rewrite it. The programmer continually evaluates all programs and makes adjustments as necessary. This low rate of job growth can lead a decrease in employment. However, it's a rewarding job that you can do at home and alone. As a programmer, you will help to develop a web-based system for information and also develop, test, and implement computer programs on different operating systems. They verify the program's operation through tests, and also create and publish technical drawings to show the effects of coding.

To progress as a programmer and to be successful, you will need the following skills. Reading skills, problem solving skills, critical thinking skills and active listening are all essential. It is important to know your personality type, work-related interests and values. This job requires a computer science degree. You also need a computer with high speed internet service. An hourly wage of $40 is the norm. Refer to freelancer.com for more information.

Growth

* You will need $500 to begin, but if there is a computer and high speed internet, you can start with $500.

* It will take 3 months to build and you will need courses to help you learn more as you move up the ranks.

* You can get a raise in your hourly rate from $40 to 60

* You can hire a virtual assistant

Here are some helpful links

* You can see videos related the job in YouTube

* Freelancer.com can be your first job.

* You may apply for Udemy training programs after some time. Then, you can apply in Flexjobs.com

Pros and cons for a Programmer

Pros

* This job is in high demand

* Steady income

* Education is not very important

* Insurance and other benefit packages available

* Positive working conditions

Cons

* Boring work may be possible

* Sitting at a desk in front of the computer

* You have to do everything, including configuration and coding. It can be stressful.

REALTOR

A Realtor is an agent or broker who is licensed and a member of The National Association of Realtors. Some realtors are agents while others are brokers. Managers of an agency who have agents under them as salespeople are called brokers. They must pay additional fees to keep their state-issued brokerage license. The written test for real estate agents is taken by those who are licensed to be realtors. Each realtor must strictly follow the code of ethics. Clients will feel more secure knowing that they have worked with highly vetted agents, and that they have sworn up to their professional standards.

As realtors, your duties are to maintain client funds apart, cooperate with other agents and broker if it is in their client's best interests, promote clients' interests above their own, treat all parties fairly, get consent from the client before accepting any form payment or commission. Working 40 hours per week is possible and you can earn $20 an hour. You also get sell-on commissions. For your first job, you'll need a computer with internet service and a dedicated telephone. You also need a NAR licence and a designated area at home. As average realtors, they get a 3% Commission on each sale and make $45,990 annually. Flexjobs.com offers a useful link.

Growth

* Starting with $700 is a good starting point, but you can work with less if you have high-speed Internet and a computer.

* It takes two months to create, and you must take courses to continue your education.

* You can get a raise in your hourly rate from $20 to $65,

Here are some helpful links

* You can see videos related the job in YouTube

* You may start with Fiverr.com

* After some time, you can apply for Udemy training programs and apply in Flexjobs.com

There are pros and cons to being a realtor

Pros

* You have the freedom to set your own schedule.

* You have the potential for a high income

* You will help your clients achieve their dreams

Cons

* It can be stressful and frustrating for both sides

* The job is contingent on commission

* Working more than your set hours might be possible if there aren't any.

REPAIRER

A repairer is a skilled person who works to fix things. Someone who can fix things using darning. They can be maintenance, repair or menders. There is a great need for handymen all over the world. It is important to decide what repair skills you are able to offer to make a living as a home-based contractor. It is profitable to specialize in a specific repair skill, even though you may be able do everything. A repairer can provide a wide range of services. It is important to make a list with the possible services you provide. Know your area's repairer laws before starting a business.

You need to find out what services you can offer and not be allowed to do so. For the service that you plan to offer, make sure you get the license. Find customers to start with and work your way up. Focus on the customer you are serving and design your business around them. Some customers will pay higher rates, provided you do a great work. Others may want the lowest rates. Your business will prosper if it targets the right customers.

The main reason you apply for a job is to set your pricing. A repairer may earn between $50 and $100 per hour. It is possible to be extremely profitable if the price is right. If you are setting a price, make sure it is affordable enough to make a profit. This is especially important when starting a repair company. A market strategy is what you need to be able get clients. There are many repairmen, so you need to have a strategy that can outshine them all. It all comes down how and what you offer them. A license, repair software and liability insurance are all you need to begin this business. Flexjobs.com is a useful link.

Growth

* You will need $400 to begin, but if there is high-speed Internet and a computer, you can start with $0

* It will take about a month to build, and you will need to take courses to improve your skills.

* You have the option to increase your hourly wage from $50 to $145

Here are some helpful links

* You can see videos related the job in YouTube

* You may start with Fiverr.com

* After some time, you can apply for Udemy training programs and then apply to Flexjobs.com

There are pros and cons to a repairer

Pros

It can be fun, and it can also be very profitable.

* High levels of job security

* Making your customers happy.

Cons

* It may take some time before you make a profit

* There may be distractions

It can be stressful

TRANSCRIBER

A transcription job is one of the most highly-sought-after online jobs. You can find a job as a transcriber even from your home, provided you have the required skills and equipment. The foot pedal and the transcription software allow transcribers to convert video and audio files into text. The task can take up to an hour. The first step to becoming a home-based transcriber is to purchase a computer, high speed internet service, transcription software and a foot pedal. Test your typing speed with a good transcription software. A key skill is the ability to retain spoken words accurately and not lose their meaning.

Learn about your foreign accents. You can purchase a quality headset with noise reduction and audio booster. If you are faced with an inaudible file, it is a good idea to have a working knowledge of audio processing. Once you have completed this information, you can apply online to a home-based job in transcription. Earn $25-30 an hour. Fiverr.com offers a helpful link.

Growth

* Start with $500, but with a computer and high speed internet you can work with less.

It will take approximately three months to build and you will need courses to help you learn more as you go.

* You can get a raise in your hourly rate from $30 to $60

Here are some helpful links

* You can see videos related the job in YouTube

* You may start with Fiverr.com

* After some time, you can apply for Udemy training programs and apply in Flexjobs.com

A Transcriber's Pros and Cones

Pros

* You have the option to accept or decline projects at your own discretion

* You choose your hours

* You will be able save money

Cons

* There are many stress factors involved in trying to find a job.

* Boring due to isolation

* You must keep track of your income as well as expenses

EDITING

Editing is something you do right after you have finished your first draft. Your draft is reviewed to determine if it is well-organized, if the paragraph changes are seamless, and whether your evidence backs up your argument. You can modify your overall structure, content style, clarity, and number of citations. Glassdoor states that an online editor earns between $15 and $50 per hour and averages $51,104 per year. As more online publications offer subcontract editing services, the demand for editors is strong. Self-published authors also require professional editing of their manuscripts. You will need to have a computer and high speed internet.

An editor doesn't necessarily need to be educated, but they need to know the basics of grammar, punctuation, style and spelling. The first step is to choose the type and price of editing you want, set up a business and obtain the necessary permits and licenses. Next, you need to establish your business presence, market your company, find clients, and create a business plan. This job is in high demand. Fiverr.com can be a good resource.

Growth

*You will need $600 to begin, but if there is a computer and high speed internet access, you can start with far less.

It will take you three to develop and you will need courses to help you learn more as you move up the ranks.

* You have the option to increase your hourly rate from $15 to $65

Here are some helpful links

* You can see videos related the job in YouTube

* You may start with Fiverr.com

* Apply in Flexjobs.com for Udemy-approved training courses.

Pros and cons of Editing

Pros

* You can also specialize

* You can always work

* You can do work anywhere

Cons

* Your income is unpredictable

* It is not simple to get clients

* It'd be a great help to have lots of discipline

PROOFREADING

The last part of the editing process is proofreading. Here you will focus on surface errors such misspellings and grammar mistakes. Proofreading should be done after all other editing has been completed. A lot of people dedicate a few minutes to proofreading. They want to catch any obvious errors that leap out at them. However, even after spending hours working on a paper, a quick and cursory reading can sometimes miss a lot. It is much better to use a specific plan which allows you to search carefully for certain types of errors.

While it may take a bit more time, the results are worth it. Knowing that there is an efficient way to fix errors once the paper has been completed will allow you to focus on writing your first drafts. This makes it easier to write well. You should keep editing and proofreading separate. It is important to not spend time worrying about grammar, punctuation and spelling while editing drafts. It's not helpful to worry about spelling or where to place a comma. This distracts you from the important task at hand: developing and linking ideas.

Proofreaders, just like editors in the publishing world, require an acute eye for detail. You can work remotely as a proofreader. To do this, you need to understand the work scope and find your niche. After that, you should invest in yourself. You will need a computer with internet access. Proofreaders earn between $30 and $50 an hour. This is a demanding job with high growth rates. Fiverr.com is an excellent resource.

Growth

*You will need $600 to begin, but if there is a computer and high speed internet access, you can start with less.

* This will take 3 months to build and you will need courses to help you learn more as you move up the ranks.

* You have the ability to raise your hourly wage from $30 to $70

Here are some helpful links

* You can see videos related the job in YouTube

* You may start with Fiverr.com

* You may apply in Flexjobs.com for Udemy-trained courses after a while.

Pros and cons of proofreading

Pros

* You can also specialize

* You can do work anywhere

* You can always work

Cons

* Your income is unpredictable

* It would be helpful if you were very disciplined

* It isn't easy to find clients

VIRTUAL RECUITER

Virtual recruiters share the same goals and responsibilities that traditional recruiters. You are there to help potential job candidates fill their vacancies. Virtual recruiters usually work from home and are not based in the office. This part is about connecting potential employers and job-seekers. It helps narrow down the field of qualified job candidates, while helping job seekers to find the right match. Since you are not present in the office, clients will receive regular updates via emails, phone and online about your search status. Recruitment jobs are often remote and virtual.

A virtual recruiter who works from home searches for qualified candidates to fill their client's job openings. To identify candidates who meet your client's requirements, you use social media to search job boards and other relevant websites. Most home-based recruiting firms conduct an initial screening by phone with the job applicant.

Then, they may meet in person and forward the job seeker's information to their client. Virtual recruiters from home can often earn a commission if the client hires their candidate.

Virtual recruiters can work from their home but do not need to have any formal education. However, most have a high-school diploma. Employers will sometimes prefer applicants who have a bachelor's degree in human resource, business, marketing, and related subjects. As a customer service representative or salesperson, you can begin your career and develop your communication skills. It is essential that you are able to search and navigate social media sites and other websites in order be a great virtual recruiter. Basic computer programming skills are essential, as well as being self-motivated. A computer with high speed internet access and space for storage would be an advantage. It is possible to earn an hourly salary of $35 and this job is highly in demand. Fiverr.com offers a helpful link.

Growth

*You will need $600 to begin, but if there is a computer and high speed internet access, then you can start with a lot less.

* It takes one month to build, and you'll need courses to help you learn more as your skills improve.

* Your hourly rate can go up from $35 to $60

Here are some helpful links

* You can see videos related the job in YouTube

* You may start with Fiverr.com

* After some time, you can apply for Udemy training programs and apply to Flexjobs.com

There are pros and cons to using a virtual recruiter

Pros

* It has a high potential to pay

* Get paid for your results by a commission

* You can have flexibility and control your own time

* It is a great place to grow professionally

* You will develop valuable sales skills

Cons

* You must manage the risks yourself

* You are not off the clock

* Recruiting a sales job

* There is Competition

FILM & POST INSTRUCTIONAL VIDEOS

An instructional video is a video which demonstrates or transfers knowledge.

Instructional videos can be made by anyone, not just instructional designers. It's not the case anymore. Instructive videos are possible for anyone, from any industry. There are many types of instructional videos that you can make, including micro-videos. These videos focus on a particular topic and are easy to create. Tutorial videos show someone how to do something. Training videos are designed to help people improve their work skills. You can also make explainer videos, screencasts videos, or presentation videos. Be sure to know your audience before creating videos. Make sure you are making the videos useful. You don't want to create perfect videos, but instead a video that teaches. To create videos, you don't necessarily need fancy equipment. But the right tools can help you achieve your goals. This is how you can create a screen-recorded video. Get to know your audience, create a script, record the narration, then record the screen. Add a video intro and edits. Start with a few tools: a tripod, smartphone and phone clip. A 1000-view video can cost you $1 to $2. Fiverr.com offers a useful link.

Growth

* Starting with $700 is a good starting point, but you can work with less if you have high-speed Internet and a computer.

It will take approximately three months to create, and you will need courses to continue your education.

* You can increase the amount you receive from $1000 up to $2000 per viewing.

Here are some helpful links

* You can see videos related the job in YouTube

* You may start with Fiverr.com

* After some time, you can apply for Udemy training programs and then apply in Flexjobs.com

The Pros and Cons Of Filming and Publishing Instructional Videos

Pros

* You can discover new ideas

* Very comfortable

* Easy to create

Cons

* It is possible to be boring

* It can be expensive to get started

* It's hard to get viewers

PRODUCT REVIEWER

A product reviewer refers to someone who reviews products for a company. There are many businesses that offer product testing. You must review the products and fill out a survey once you have. You think this sounds like a straightforward way to get some free stuff? But it isn't. Many people are coming to these products to test them. Many who sign up to these programs don't get a response. Ask me why? It's because of the sheer number of people. Most of them are already familiar with the business and will not hesitate to give feedback. The market is constantly changing, and there could be room to hire new product testers as new products are released each month.

Before you can become a product reviewer from home, you must first identify a niche market and then review common products within that niche. For product reviews to be posted, you need a YouTube channel as well as a review blog. There are two options. One is better. You can also write product reviews. But, this will not be true if the seller has a great user community. Even if you disagree with the product, it is important to write an honest review. Honest reviews are good for both the buyer and seller. Remember that businesses may view your review as valuable feedback. It is therefore important that you do a thorough review.

To make $20 to $25 per review you'll need a space in your home that is designated for your work. Freelancer.com is an excellent resource.

Growth

* Start with $500, but with a computer and high speed internet you can work with less.

* It takes two months to create, and you must take courses to improve your skills.

* You can get a raise in your hourly rate from $20 to 50 dollars

Here are some helpful links

* You can see videos related the job in YouTube

* Freelancer.com can be your first job.

* After some time, you can apply for Udemy training programs and then apply in Flexjobs.com

Reviewers' Pros and Con of Product Reviews

Pros

* The company can make more sales

* You can offer assurances to customers

* You can make profit

* It can be adapted to your needs.

Cons

* The changing perspectives of customers

* You'll need to keep your account updated.

* This information could be harmful

VIRTUAL TOTOR

Online tutors, also known as virtual tutors, offer online tutorials to students on a range of subjects. The virtual tutor can be either a classroom instructor, or an in-person tutor. Virtual tutors respond to student messages and maintain a record. They also answer technical and connectivity questions, grade assignments, help students with homework, assist school administrators in making changes to their curriculum, and monitor student progress.

Virtual tutors have to be experts in the subjects they teach. These tutors usually have formal education and a college degree. Clients also want tutors that are skilled in their particular field.

Online tutoring programs are also available. These programs cover topics like group dynamics, listening strategies, cultural awareness, and more. Some programs have a positive impact on the business-building plans for tutors. Online tutors could choose to become professional certified or accredited by the National Tutoring Association.

The virtual tutor industry is set to experience steady job growth from 2028. Virtual tutors should complete postsecondary studies in order to be able to assist students. It is necessary to have a computer and access the internet. You can make as much as $10 an hour. Fiverr.com offers a helpful link.

Growth

* Start with $450. If you have a computer with high-speed Internet, you can start with $450.

* It takes one month to build, and you'll need courses to help you learn more as your skills improve.

* You can get a raise in your hourly rate from $10 to $40

Here are some helpful links

* You can see videos related the job in YouTube

* You may start with Fiverr.com

* After some time, you can apply for Udemy training programs and then apply in Flexjobs.com

A Virtual Tutor: The Pros and Cons

Pros

* It is convenient

* It can be used in emergencies

* There are many tutors that you can choose from

* You can digitally store and save notes

Cons

It requires greater discipline

* It works better on some subjects

It is also more expensive

* There are many scams.

VIRTUAL PUBLIC TELATIONS REPRESENTATIVE

Publicists are individuals who manage and create publicity for companies, brands or public figures for work like a film, book or album. Publicists are PR experts who manage people's image and not their entire business. Publicists are responsible for managing campaigns. Their primary focus is to get press coverage on behalf customers. They also serve as a link with clients, media outlets, and the general public. Publicists specialize in representing the public to secure maximum fees for stories sold by magazines, newspapers and television stations.

You might also be able to create your own virtual PR firm from the comfort of home. Your services may be needed if you are skilled in marketing, writing, pitching media contact management, crisis communications or planning events. Publicists require a bachelor's degree, either in journalism, communications, journalism or a related field. Publicists, like all public relations specialists, work full time with many others who work over 40 hours a week. Publicists must be comfortable with small and large groups and can conduct meetings. You can build your network and gain experience. Continue informal education. Publicists earn anywhere from $25 to $100 an hour. Freelancer.com is an excellent resource.

Growth

* You will need $500 to begin, but if there is a computer and high speed internet, you can start with less.

It will take at least two months to create, and you will need courses to continue your education.

* You can get a raise in your hourly rate from $25 to 100

* You can also hire a virtual assistant

Here are some helpful links

* You can view videos related to the job in YouTube

* Freelancer.com can be your first job.

* After some time, you can apply for Udemy training programs and apply in Flexjobs.com

A Virtual Public Relations Representative: The Pros and Cons

Pros

* It provides instant media credibility which cannot be over-stressed

* It is possible to recover from a failed program

* Improve profitability

Cons

* There is no guarantee that you'll be successful

* You can only afford what you can pay

It can be stressful

WEB SEARCH VALUATOR

Search engine evaluators help ensure that internet search results provide accurate, timely, comprehensive, and spam-free information. It is not uncommon to have a college diploma. The part-time work may include temporary employment or independent contractor status. Home-based web search evaluators need to be native speakers of the languages they are working in, have an understanding of the internet, and be familiarized with a large number of online news sources. They can work anywhere from four to six hour days per week. They will need to be able web researcher and analytical skills as well as a wide range of interests that include expertise.

There are three steps to getting started as a Web Search Evaluator. You must apply to one the companies hiring them, complete the paperwork, and pass the qualification test. If you are hardworking, you can make $1000 a months. You will need a smartphone, computer, internet service with high speed and active Gmail. The job is in high demand. Fiverr.com can be a good link.

Growth

* You will need $500 to begin, but if there is a computer and high speed internet, you can start with $500.

* It takes two months to create, and you must take courses to improve your skills.

* You can increase the amount you earn from $1000 to 1500 per month.

Here are some helpful links

* You can see videos related the job in YouTube

* You may start with Fiverr.com

* You may apply for Udemy training programs after some time. Then, you can apply to Flexjobs.com.

Web Search Evaluation: Pros and cons

Pros

* It can be adapted to your needs.

It's a great way of making huge amounts of cash.

* You don't necessarily need to program code

* This job is done from the comfort of home

Cons

* It can be stressful

* It is impossible to guarantee clients or profits

It can be frustrating and monotonous.

WEBSITE TESTER

Website testers are responsible primarily for monitoring and testing websites, web applications, and other devices on multiple laptops, desktops and mobile devices. They must have programming skills and be detail-oriented. They are expected to ensure user satisfaction by certifying that the final product meets client needs. They may be contracted for part-time or permanent work. Testing functional systems, ensuring end users are satisfied, working collaboratively with developers, recording all testing results, training junior website testers, and documenting them are some of the duties of a website tester. They will need to be able to manage their time and have technical skills, problem-solving skills as well interpersonal skills.

You'll need a computer and software. As the demand is high, you could earn up to $14.90 per an hour. Fiverr.com offers a helpful link.

Growth

* You will need $500 to begin, but if there is a computer and high speed internet, you can start with $500.

* It will take at least two months for you to build it, and you'll need courses to help you learn more as you go.

* You can get a raise in your hourly rate from $15 to 50 dollars

Here are some helpful links

* You can see videos related the job in YouTube

* You may start with Fiverr.com

* After some time, you can apply for Udemy training programs and then apply in Flexjobs.com

Website tester: The pros and cons

Pros

* It is right

It is also profitable

* No advanced certificate required

Cons

It is more boring than social.

* It is very difficult to start

* You need many skills

SHORT TASKS

These short task sites offer a way to make quick cash online. However, like any other crowdsourced earning opportunity, there are pros as well as cons. A short task is a website where crowdsourced employees perform small tasks. Although the task site's set-up and job offerings may differ, they can all be used in the same way. It is common for both the seller and buyer of services to agree on the execution and payment of a particular task. It could be either the buyer or seller who advertised the task.

www.ingramcontent.com/pod-product-compliance
Lightning Source LLC
Chambersburg PA
CBHW071220210326
41597CB00016B/1887